Dr George Chryssides is Senior Lecturer in Religious Studies at the University of Wolverhampton, England and a practising Unitarian.

D0167057

The *Elements of* is a series designed to present high-quality introductions to a broad range of essential subjects.

The books are commissioned specifically from experts in their fields. They provide readable and often unique views of the various topics covered, and are therefore of interest both to those who have some knowledge of the subject, as well as to those who are approaching it for the first time.

Many of these concise yet comprehensive books have practical suggestions and exercises which allow personal experience as well as theoretical understanding, and offer a valuable source of information on many important themes.

In the same series

The Aborigine Tradition	Human Potential
Alchemy	The I Ching
The Arthurian Tradition	Islam
Astrology	Judaism
The Bahá'í Faith	Meditation
Buddhism	Mysticism
Celtic Christianity	Native American Traditions
The Celtic Tradition	Natural Magic
The Chakras	Numerology
Christian Symbolism	Pendulum Dowsing
Creation Myth	Prophecy
Dreamwork	Psychosynthesis
The Druid Tradition	The Qabalah
Earth Mysteries	Reincarnation
Egyptian Wisdom	The Runes
Feng Shui	Shamanism
Gnosticism	Sufism
The Goddess	Tai Chi
The Grail Tradition	Taoism
Graphology	The Tarot
Handreading	Visualisation
Herbalism	World Religions
Hinduism	Yoga
	Zen

the elements of

unitarianism

George D Chryssides

ELEMENT

Shaftesbury, Dorset • Boston, Massachusetts • Melbourne, Victoria

© Element Books Limited 1998
Text © George D Chryssides 1998

First published in Great Britain in 1998 by
Element Books Limited
Shaftesbury, Dorset SP7 8BP

Published in the USA in 1998 by
Element Books, Inc.
160 North Washington St, Boston MA 02114

Published in Australia in 1998 by
Element Books and distributed by
Penguin Australia Limited
487 Maroondah Highway
Ringwood, Victoria 3134

All rights reserved.
No part of this book may be reproduced or
utilized in any form or by any means, electronic
or mechanical, without prior permission in
writing from the Publisher.

Cover design by Max Fairbrother
Design by Roger Lightfoot
Typeset by Backup Creative Services
Dorset DT10 1DB
Printed and bound in Great Britain by
Biddles Ltd, Guildford, Kings Lynn

British Library Cataloguing in Publication
data available

Library of Congress Cataloguing in Publication
data
Chryssides, George D., 1945
The elements of Unitarianism
George D. Chryssides
p. cm.
Includes bibliographical references and index.
ISBN 1 86204–247–0 (alk. paper)
1. Unitarianism. I. Title
BX984–.2.C48 1988
289. 1— dc.21
97–39390 CIP

ISBN 1 86204 247 0

CONTENTS

DEDICATION

To the Unitarian congregation at Notte Street, Plymouth,
England, who first introduced me to Unitarianism

PREFACE

This book was originally commissioned by the Hibbert Trustees, who felt that the time was right for a new book on the Unitarians. They had sponsored John Hostler's book *Unitarianism* which appeared in 1981, and which is still prized by many Unitarians. Hostler is now out of print, and in the meantime things have moved on in the denomination.

My particular brief was specially to focus on Unitarianism's inter-faith work, to which I have tried to give substantial coverage, but more generally to provide an introduction to the Unitarian faith which would, as the trustees put it, 'gently commend it' to outsiders. The second aim meant that it would be unproductive simply to use the denomination's own Lindsey Press, which distributes literature mainly within the movement; a wider circulation needed an outside commercial publisher. The *Elements of* series seemed ideal, covering a wide variety of religious ways of life, all written by practising exponents.

Commercial publishers invariably look to an American market to boost sales and, as a result, I had rapidly to increase my acquaintance with Unitarianism in the USA and Canada. The Hibbert Trustees were sufficiently generous to fly me out to Spokane in 1995 to attend the Unitarian Universalist General Assembly that summer. The American dimension has caused some shift to the book's centre of gravity, which may be no bad thing. American books on the Unitarians have tended to focus on America, British ones on Britain, with hardly anything on Transylvania. Only E M Wilbur's rather daunting two-volume *A History of Unitarianism* (1946 and 1952) attempts to paint a global picture.

Because of its scope, the treatment of certain topics and people has had to be unduly swift. No doubt there are readers who will look for their favourite Unitarian cause or hero, only to be disappointed. My aim has been to identify key events and follow general trends.

I have attempted to be politically correct by using inclusive language throughout, but I hope that readers will appreciate that in some cases this is just not possible, particularly when quoting older Unitarian writings. Although I have agonized about how to refer to God in a genderless way, the circumlocutions that this might entail could have had the effect of distorting what Unitarians of the past were saying. I can only ask the reader to bear with this, and to remember that not all Unitarians are PC, as will become apparent!

Numerous friends and colleagues have given their time, advice and assistance. This has been much appreciated. My thanks are due to Dick and Jopie Boeke, Robin Boyes, Eila Forrester, Jeremy and Rosemary Goring, Andrew Hill, Frank Hytch, Joan Lamb and Vernon Marshall. I am grateful to Matthew Smith and Ingrid Tavkar at the British headquarters for answering numerous inquiries and providing information. Colleagues at the University of Wolverhampton, England, have discussed some of this material in the course of post-graduate seminars, and I should like to thank Deirdre Burke, Ron Geaves and Joyce Miller for their useful comments.

Thanks too are due to Jim McClelland and the Hibbert Trustees, who have taken an interest throughout the book's preparation, and have been very patient in awaiting its outcome. The staff at Dr Williams's Library have been most helpful in searching out improbable books. I have also benefited greatly from fellow Unitarians who have taken the trouble to put information about the movement, and about their favourite themes on the Internet: this has saved me much searching.

Special thanks are due to the Unitarians of Romania and Hungary, whose help and hospitality were truly impressive. Conversations with Ilona Szent-Iványi Orbók and Bishop Arpad Szábo provided invaluable insights into the distinctive aspects of Transylvanian Unitarianism. The late Bishop John Erdö deserves thanks for answering questions, and for showing me and other IARF (International Association for Religious Freedom) members around Kolozsvár, during a recent visit: his recent death is a great loss to the movement. I am grateful to John Storey for permission to quote his hymn, 'Religion needs to permeate'.

This book could not have been written if had not been for Richard Lovis and other friends at the Unitarian Church at Notte Street, Plymouth, England, who welcomed me into the movement, and made me feel at home as a member there.

Finally, my wife Margaret has listened to most of these ideas, read drafts and provided invaluable suggestions and information, as well as support throughout the book's writing.

INTRODUCTION

I first became aware of the Unitarians as an undergraduate in Glasgow. The Saturday edition of *The Glasgow Herald* carried classified advertisements for the local churches. These were divided into three principal sections: the Church of Scotland congregations, Roman Catholics, and a third section which contained an assortment of spiritual groups spanning Christian Science, the Swedenborgians, the Seventh Day Adventists and various Spiritualist organizations – groups which appeared to be 'on the fringes' of Christianity. The Unitarians fell into this 'assorted' section.

The term 'Unitarian' connoted a contrast with 'Trinitarian', and some of my acquaintances, who seemed reasonably well informed about such matters, assured me that, 'They're the ones who deny the Trinity'. Other friends offered additional explanations, such as, 'They don't believe in the divinity of Christ', 'They deny the existence of the Holy Spirit', or that they were cold rationalists devoid of any feelings of spirituality.

I had been brought up to attend the Church of Scotland faithfully and, having become a loyal member at the age of 16, I found it hard to understand why anyone should seek spiritual solace in a minority religious group. So important did my church seem, that I decided that I would train for the ministry. This involved reading for a first degree in philosophy at a university, and then spending a further three years studying divinity.

My vague opinions about the Unitarians were slightly revised in my final year as a philosophy student at Glasgow University. I had come to know a teacher from India, a Hindu by birth, who had recently settled in Scotland. We became friends and, in exchange for hospitality which my family provided from time to time, Mr Patel initiated us in Indian-style dining in one or other of Glasgow's newly established Indian restaurants. Mr Patel, who described himself as a 'Hindu Christian', had come to know the city's Unitarian congregation. Because of my own mainstream church connections at the time, I never accompanied him to a Unitarian service, but I once dropped in with him one evening, when he needed to deliver a message to two of the members, to whom I was introduced. The meeting which they were attending was connected with the newly founded Amnesty International, and they explained something about Amnesty's work to me. They certainly appeared to be much more concerned about political and social involvement than I had been led to believe. Obviously, too, the congregation provided an acceptable bridge between Hinduism and Christianity for my Indian friend.

I completed my philosophy degree successfully, and progressed to Trinity College in Glasgow. At last I had achieved my ambition of being able to devote all my time to the subject which had always interested me the most – religion! However, my adolescent certainties became replaced by serious doubts. How could Jesus be divine and human simultaneously? What sense could be attached to saying that Christ was 'eternally begotten of the Father before all worlds'? How could someone's crucifixion 2,000 years ago atone for the sins of the entire human race?

When I used to air such doubts to friends, they would sometimes tell me that I should not be offering myself for the Christian ministry. I suspected that they might be right! After all, many of the hymns and prayers with which I had become familiar suggested strongly that doubt was a sin: 'We will never doubt thee', and 'Our doubts and fears remove' were lines of popular hymns which I had frequently sung from my childhood. I decided, together with one other student who had similar problems, that I was unable to offer myself as a candidate for the ministry. We both took the unusual step of refusing to sign the Church of Scotland's declaration of faith and, having collected our Bachelor of Divinity degrees, we both sought careers in the world of education instead.

I continued to attend church after moving to Plymouth in England, and sought membership of a local United Reformed Church. This involved a service of admission in which the new member was presented to the congregation. The minister, no doubt with the best of intentions, based his sermon on 1 Corinthians 12, where Paul talks about the Church being one body, consisting of many parts, just as the human body has different parts.

> The eye cannot say to the hand, 'I don't need you!' And the head cannot say to the feet, 'I don't need you!' (1 Corinthians 12. 21)

The gist of the sermon was that, although some might question my place in the Church, I still had one. It sounded a somewhat grudging acceptance, and I did not appreciate it!

Several years after that incident I met up with the Plymouth Unitarians. My first visit to the Notte Street chapel was on a Saturday afternoon for an inter-faith gathering, addressed by the local rabbi and a Zen Buddhist amongst others. I realized once again that Unitarians were interested in a variety of faiths.

Some time later the congregation's minister left. Having heard that I had once undergone ministerial training, the secretary asked if I would be willing to conduct a service during the vacancy. I was slightly surprised that they should ask an outsider, but I agreed. I cannot recall what I preached about but, when I was invited back, I sought a second opinion from a mainstream Christian minister on whether I should accept. 'Preach to them about the Trinity!' he advised. I consulted a number of scholarly works on the Trinity, and presented the Plymouth congregation with a sermon which explained mainstream Christianity's understanding of the doctrine, as well as some popular misconceptions on the subject. After the service, one member remarked, 'It was an interesting sermon, but these matters don't really bother Unitarians very much now!'

On a further occasion the same person remarked that some of the members were finding my prayers problematic. I was puzzled at first, since I had always taken the trouble to ensure that the prayers I used were in modern language and relevant to everyday needs. However, the difficulty arose because I had concluded with the words 'through Jesus Christ our Lord' at the end of each prayer. This was my first initiation into 'non-adorationism' – the view that Jesus of Nazareth is to be respected as a teacher and an example to follow, but not someone to be invoked in one's prayers, which should straightforwardly be addressed to God.

After several pulpit invitations, I wanted to see how Unitarians themselves conducted their worship, and I started to attend Sunday services. As my acquaintance grew, Unitarianism's principal appeal to me was that it had no creed. Here was a community where doubt was no longer a vice: doubts were healthy, even to be encouraged. Here was a community that would not question my right to be part of it, or ascertain whether I was toeing a doctrinal party line. Within a short time I finally made the decision that I was a Unitarian.

Notice that I have said that I *was* a Unitarian, not that I *became* one! Many people who find their way into the Unitarians will say, like me, that their decision to join was not a conversion, but more of a recognition of what they already were. Becoming a Unitarian does not call on anyone to abandon beliefs that they have previously held, or to assume a new Unitarian creed that rivals the mainstream Trinitarian one. It does not encourage those who join to abandon their previous faith, and indeed there are those who come to Unitarian services who attend equally often at a mainstream Christian place of worship, or who have joint allegiance to some other religious group. All those who find themselves helped by Unitarian ideals or practices are welcome, with no strings attached.

Some Unitarians have similar stories to mine, about previously belonging to a mainstream denomination and coming to question some of its central teachings. Others may have seen an advertisement, read some of Unitarianism's basic literature, or spoken to someone who has mentioned the Unitarian Church, and felt attracted by its ideas. Some have found themselves passing a Unitarian chapel, decided to attend a service out of curiosity, and found themselves drawn in. Increasingly these days, with the information technology explosion, there are those who surf the net and find that, like many religious groups, the Unitarians have a presence there. Finally, there are members who are Unitarians by birth, some of whom can claim a tradition of Unitarian allegiance that extends back to five or more generations, and who are justly proud of it.

1 · HOW UNITARIANISM BEGAN

Finding the starting point of a faith that does not have a founder-leader is always something of a problem. Did Judaism, for example, begin with Moses and the Torah that was given on Mount Sinai? Or was it Abraham and the rite of circumcision? Was it King Solomon and the establishment of the Jerusalem Temple? Or was it the rise of the rabbis and the synagogue movement?

Just as there is no clear answer to the question of when Judaism began, it is not easy to ascertain who was the first Unitarian. Some might point to Theophilus Lindsey (1723–1808), who opened the first Unitarian chapel in London. Others might point to John Biddle (1616–62), the English clergyman who spent roughly half his life in prison for claiming that the Holy Spirit was an emanation of God, not a separate 'person'. Others might look to Transylvania, where Francis Dávid (1510–79) taught; in fact we first encounter the word 'Unitarian' in a declaration made at the Diet of Lécfalva in 1600. Some Unitarians might, slightly tongue in cheek, go further back, and nominate Moses, who wrote the words of the *shema*, 'the Lord our God, the Lord is one' (Deuteronomy 6.4), or Abraham, who firmly believed in God's oneness, or even Adam! Almost since religion began there have been men and women who affirmed the oneness of God, and Unitarians have always been proud of the affinity that this traditional fundamental belief gives them with Jews and Muslims in particular. Indeed, John Biddle was concerned that the doctrine of the Trinity – which he described as 'a three-headed Cerberus' – might make mainstream Christians the 'laughing-stock' of these other monotheistic faiths.

Perhaps the best way to understand the Unitarians is to view them as products of the Protestant Reformation. The Reformation is sometimes presented as if almost the whole of Christendom was Roman Catholic until Martin Luther came along. Luther – at least according to the version I was taught at school – was the first Protestant, after whom half of Western Christendom embraced Protestantism, while the Counter-Reformation gave rise to a semi-reformed Roman Catholic Church.

The three main issues which the Protestant Reformers addressed were the role of the Bible, the nature and number of the sacraments, and the source of authority within the Christian Church. These three issues, of course, were interconnected. Martin Luther (1483-1546) is perhaps best known for his opposition to Tetzel, the indulgence seller of Wittenburg. (Indulgences were special favours which could be purchased from authorized 'pardoners', and which were deemed to cancel out one's sins, or to assist the souls of the dead through purgatory.) Luther's disquiet at the practice of indulgences led him to pin his famous '95 Theses' to the door of the parish church at Wittenburg. Although the sale of indulgences provided the occasion for Luther's action, the Theses went much further than mere criticism of the practice itself. Luther had revisited the Bible, and noted that the apostle Paul rejected 'works' as the means of salvation, whether this meant buying indulgences to expiate sin, doing works of charity, or receiving the sacrament of the Mass. No priesthood, no fellowship of saints, no blessed Virgin Mary might intercede with God on behalf of the Christian; each individual was his or her own 'priest', in accordance with Luther's principle of 'the priesthood of all believers'.

However, this is barely adequate as an account of what was really taking place within the Christian Church. Not all the Reformers had the same religious agenda by any means, but they argued amongst themselves, sometimes acrimoniously.

Luther was certainly not the first Church leader to suggest the reforms for which he is so often given the credit. The scholar Desiderius Erasmus (c1469-1536) had already criticized the superstition which surrounded the Mass and had ridiculed the Church's institutions in his celebrated work, *In Praise of Folly*. Erasmus had also turned his attention to the Bible, reading the New Testament in its original Greek instead of the more popular Latin Vulgate. He became the first Professor of Greek at the University of Cambridge.

In their rejection of papal authority, the Reformers had suggested that over the centuries a large accretion of doctrines and practices had developed that did not have their basis in scripture. The traditional creeds were further examples of this. Did the Bible really support the idea, as the creeds stated, that Jesus was simultaneously fully human and fully divine, or that God was three persons in one? And if Jesus was *not* fully divine, should he be addressed in prayer, or should Christians exclusively direct their devotion to God the Father? These discussions did not feature in the deliberations of the best known Reformers, such as Martin Luther and John Calvin (1509–64). In fact Calvin, in his *Institutes of the Christian Religion,* simply assumed that the Bible supported the doctrines of the creeds, and purported to demonstrate this by copious notes giving 'proof texts' for the doctrines of the Incarnation and the Trinity. However, for a number of lesser known figures in the Protestant tradition, it could not so readily be assumed that the creeds and the Bible coincided so perfectly. A number of these Reformers were the precursors of Unitarianism, and I shall give a few thumbnail sketches of famous 'Unitarians' who lived around the time of the Protestant Reformation. Some of these debates may, in hindsight, seem obscure and irrelevant to the 20th and 21st century reader, and it is therefore important to emphasize, as subsequent chapters will make clear, that Unitarian thinking has moved on considerably from that of its founder figures.

FRANCIS DÁVID (DÁVID FERENC) (1510–79)

Francis Dávid – known to Hungarian speakers as Dávid Ferenc, on account of the Hungarian practice of placing one's surname first – was born in Kolozsvár in Transylvania. (The city is now called Cluj, and forms part of modern Romania.) In 1566 he gained the position of court preacher to King John Sigismund. In the spirit of the Reformation, Dávid was convinced that scripture alone, and in particular the Christian gospels, yielded religious truth. Giorgio Blandrata (c1518–85), John Sigismund's physician, persuaded Dávid that if one read the Judaeo-Christian scriptures aright, one must conclude that they taught the unity of God and not the Trinity.

In the same year Dávid was appointed as Bishop of the Calvinist community in Kolozsvár, where he regularly preached at the Great Church. Dávid began to preach about the oneness of God and against the Trinity. The Trinity, he contended, was a later addition on the part of the Church, coming from a few of its general councils, who were influenced by the Greek philosophy that was prevalent in their times. Not only did Dávid believe that the doctrine of the Trinity was unscriptural: it was unintelligible also. If salvation really depended on acceptance of the doctrine, then, Dávid argued, the average Transylvanian peasant was doomed! As Dávid once wrote:

> We are judged to be heretics because we can no longer believe
> in essence, person, nature, incarnation, as they want us to
> believe. If these things are necessary for salvation, it is certain
> that no poor peasant Christian is saved, because he could never
> understand them in all his life.[1]

If God was one, then it followed that Jesus was not God. Dávid, however, was prepared to accept that Jesus was the son of God, the saviour of humanity, the judge of all the world, the head of the Church, and even that he was born of a virgin, since scripture clearly taught the Virgin Birth. Those who believed in Christ could achieve new birth through the Holy Spirit. Later in his life, Dávid went further and taught that prayer should be addressed directly to God, not through Jesus Christ, and that the Holy Spirit was God's sanctifying spirit or energy.

The Great Church of Kolozsvár, in which Dávid regularly preached, still stands to this day, and is a memorial his work. Somewhat ironically, however, it was taken over by the Roman Catholic Church in the eighteenth century, and is currently used by them.

MICHAEL SERVETUS (1511–53)

A second early precursor of Unitarians was a contemporary of Francis Dávid: Michael Servetus. Born in Navarre in southern France, Servetus was brought up as a Roman Catholic. When he went to university, he read the Bible for the first time, and concluded that the traditional creeds and confessions were not wholly founded on scripture. In common with Dávid, Servetus was unable to accept the doctrine of the Trinity as biblically based.

Servetus believed that if the Jews and the Muslims were to be converted to Christianity, Christian teaching on the Trinity had to be revised. Christianity's most serious error, he believed, was the doctrine of the 'eternal existence of the Son'. Servetus wrote two important treatises, *Errors of the Trinity* and *Dialogues on the Trinity*. Jesus Christ, he claimed, was not to be equated with God; he was, rather, the supreme revealer of God, and therefore God made him divine as a special 'gift'.

In the wake of his writings, Servetus was hotly pursued by the Spanish Inquisition, and in order to escape he disguised himself, assuming the name of Michael de Villeneuve. To compete his transformation, he sought a change of career and took up the study of medicine in France. Servetus proved to be as distinguished a physician as he had been a theologian: he became physician to the Archbishop of Vienna, and he suggested a theory of the circulation of the blood which pre-dated the (Unitarian) scientist William Harvey.

Servetus did not abandon theology, however. He wrote a further work entitled *The Restitution of Christianity*, which he published anonymously in 1553, having previously sent parts of the draft to the Reformer John Calvin in Geneva. Suspicion grew that Servetus was the author, and the Inquisition sought his arrest. Servetus escaped to Geneva, but his ideas fared no better under Calvin, who had him apprehended and ordered him to be burned at the stake the same year.

Although Servetus' theology was still a far cry from Unitarianism as we know it today, he contributed a number of ideas which are still highly treasured by modern Unitarians. His determination to secure freedom of religious enquiry is particularly found and prized in contemporary Unitarian circles, as is his willingness to subject his ideas to open debate.

FAUSTUS SOCINUS (1539–1604)

A third Unitarian fountainhead is Faustus Socinus. As one modern Unitarian writer states, 'More than any other person, Faustus Socinus ... was the architect of modern Unitarianism' (Parke, p24). Unitarians are sometimes labelled as 'Socinians', a term which refers to Faustus Socinus' teaching that Jesus saved men and women, not by some mysterious atoning transaction which was accomplished on the cross, but rather by his life and example, which people might follow.

Faustus was an Italian who settled in Poland in 1579, where he became leader of the Polish Church (sometimes called the 'Polish brethren') in Cracow, a denomination which had 300 congregations and whose theology was already Unitarian. Like Servetus, Socinus' preaching and writing emphasized the humanity of Jesus, and taught that God was a unity, not a trinity. Since Jesus was not God, he did not atone for humankind as a substitutionary sacrifice for the sin of the world; Christ's saving work was essentially his teaching and the example he set for the rest of humanity to follow. Socinus' teaching caused an uproar with the masses, and in 1598 he was forced to flee the country after university students attempted to kill him.

A draft piece of writing by Socinus, entitled *The Institute of the Christian Religion*, probably formed the basis of the Racovian Catechism, which was published at Racow, in Poland, in 1605. A 'catechism' is a set of theological questions and answers on the fundamentals of the Christian faith, as understood by the relevant Protestant denomination. Anyone seeking membership of the Church might be questioned on it, and must respond verbatim with the catechism's official answers.

Like other catechisms, the Racovian Catechism was set out in question-and-answer format but, unlike its later Protestant counterparts, it was not intended to be doctrinally binding. It was a body of opinion for consideration, which might point seekers on the right path towards eternal life. The Catechism affirmed that Christian scripture was the sole source of authority, that knowledge and a 'holy life' were the means of salvation, and that God was one, not three.

Regarding Jesus, the Catechism affirmed that he lived a remarkable life, but was nonetheless a man: Christ's deity was 'repugnant not only to sound Reason, but also to the holy Scriptures'.[2] Jesus was not a mere man, however: the Catechism affirmed that he was 'conceived by the Holy Spirit', born of a virgin, that he worked miracles, and that God raised him from the dead. The resurrection was therefore God's vindication of Jesus' pure life, enabling Jesus to act as the intermediary between God and humanity; Jesus thus became the 'high priest' described in the Letter to the Hebrews, and so Christ became 'divine by office, rather than by nature'.

John Biddle (1616–62)

An English version of the Racovian Catechism was published by an English clergyman called John Biddle, and it appeared in Amsterdam in 1652. Biddle had already earned himself a reputation as a radical Reformer, and had found himself on the wrong side of the law on this account. In line with the Protestants of his time, Biddle accepted the authority of scripture; consequently, on matters regarding the Trinity and the Incarnation, his fundamental concern was what the Bible taught on such questions, rather than the ancient creeds and confessions of the historical Church.

Biddle concluded that Jesus was not God himself, nor was the Holy Spirit to be identified with God, but that in some sense Christ and the Holy Spirit were somehow divine personalities. This may seem as bewildering as some of the orthodox Trinitarianism of the less controversial scholars of his day but, like many others, Biddle was struggling to maintain the doctrine of the unity of God in the context of the inerrancy of scripture.

In 1647 Biddle published '*Twelve Questions* or Arguments drawn out of Scripture, wherein the commonly received Opinion touching the Deity of the Holy Spirit is clearly and fully refuted'. He is said to have known the scriptures so well that he knew the New Testament by heart in both English and Greek, apart from the last few chapters! In *Twelve Questions* he used his detailed knowledge of scripture, combined with close logical argument, to demonstrate, not that the Holy Spirit did not exist, but that it existed independently from God and Jesus Christ. Biddle was imprisoned, and in the same year the *Twelve Questions* were ordered to be burnt by the hangman, as blasphemous writings.

Biddle spent much of his life in custody for his writings. When Oliver Cromwell came to power in 1652, Parliament passed a general 'Act of Oblivion', restoring Biddle and others to freedom. For the next two years Biddle and his friends were able to meet each Sunday for the purpose of expounding the scriptures. This was not a formal church service, since dissenting worship was forbidden by law; one way to circumvent legislation was to form a house group which met for discussion.

It was during these two years that Biddle translated and published some of the Socinians' writings. In 1654, he published his 'Two-fold Catechism', an anti-Trinitarian rival

to 'The Larger Catechism' and 'The Shorter Catechism', both
of which were compiled in 1048 by the Westminster divines
for the national mainstream Churches in Scotland, England
and Ireland. In common with the Larger and Shorter
Catechisms, Biddle's second, shorter version of his catechism
was aimed at children. Biddle was once again arrested and
imprisoned and, after several more years of detention, finally
died in prison in 1662.

PROTESTANT DISSENTERS IN BRITAIN

The year 1662 witnessed another important event in British
religious history. At the instigation of Charles II, Parliament
passed the Act of Uniformity, which made the use of the
Church of England's Prayer Book compulsory throughout
England. (The Prayer Book remained in general use until very
recent times, when it was finally superseded by the 1980
Alternative Services Book.) Although most clergy complied,
some 2,000 refused to use it, and were consequently 'ejected'
from their parishes. This event is known as 'The Great
Ejection', and the dissenting clergy and their supporters form
the beginning of the 'Non-conformists'. The two main Non-
conformist groups which emerged were the Presbyterians and
the Congregationalists. The latter leaned towards Calvinism,
with its belief that Jesus Christ merely died to save 'the elect',
whereas the Presbyterians tended towards the belief that
Christ died for all, and that everyone had the possibility of
gaining salvation.

The notions of sin and repentance gained further
momentum with the evangelizing of John Wesley (1703-91)
and George Whitefield (1714–70), who brought Christianity to
the poorer members of the population through their open-air
preaching. Many people preferred this to the rather arid
preaching that was characteristic of the Presbyterian pulpits,
and, as a result, Presbyterianism tended to lose out. However,
there were Presbyterians who sought to ensure that a reasoned
form of Christianity – in contrast to the fiery preaching of
evangelists like Wesley – remained a live option. In 1740,
John Taylor (1694–1761), a Presbyterian minister, published

The Scripture Doctrine of Original Sin, arguing that the Calvinist doctrine of 'total depravity' was not supported by scripture. The work caused a stir, and greatly influenced what was to become Unitarian thought.

UNITARIANISM IN BRITAIN: PRIESTLEY, LINDSEY AND BELSHAM

So far we have looked at a loosely defined movement of Unitarians consisting of the above-mentioned leaders and groups of followers. In general, they had no wish to break away from mainstream Christianity, but rather hoped to persuade the Church to reap the fruits of the Protestant Reformation in a more radical way than was occurring. Unitarianism was not yet a denomination, and churches belonging to early English leaders like Biddle were not labelled 'Unitarian'.

The three people essentially responsible for establishing Unitarianism as a denomination in its own right were Joseph Priestley (1733–1804), Theophilus Lindsey (1723–1808) and Thomas Belsham (1750–1829). Priestley is generally thought of as a scientist, being the first person to isolate oxygen. (Strictly speaking, he was not its discoverer: it was left to the French chemist Lavoisier, later, to identify the gas.) However, Priestley made as great a contribution to religious thought as he did to science.

All three men shared similar aims. In the wake of new scientific discoveries, they were determined to maintain a form of religion which bore fidelity to science; and, just as science relied on reason for its conclusions so, they held, reason must be brought to bear on matters of faith, and in particular on exegesis of scripture. All three were particularly dedicated to studying the Bible, and they considered carefully the competing interpretations of the mainstream Christians, the Socinians and the Arians.[3]

Priestley's desire was to restore primitive Christianity to a Church which had, he believed, been encumbered by layers of ensuing tradition which distorted its original message. He spent six years (1782–88) writing a work entitled *History of the Corruptions of Christianity*. Priestley could not accept the Virgin Birth, and he questioned the traditional accounts of

Christ's nativity. Jesus Christ, he believed, was not divine; he was neither sinless nor infallible, nor was he predicted by the prophets (the Church, he believed, had misunderstood the nature of biblical prophecy), and beliefs in demonic possession were simply delusions belonging to his age.

Theophilus Lindsey was an Anglican clergyman who also had problems concerning Trinitarian worship. He was profoundly influenced by Paul's affirmation to the Corinthians, 'that there is but one God, the Father' (1 Corinthians 8.6). In 1774 Lindsey arrived in London, where he was helped by Priestley, who rented a room in Essex House as a temporary chapel. In April of that year the chapel was opened for public worship. This event is a significant landmark in Unitarian history, as it was the first chapel explicitly to be labelled 'Unitarian'. Under Lindsey's leadership the congregation grew dramatically. As a result it became necessary to purchase and reconstruct the Essex Street premises, part to serve as a chapel and part to provide accommodation for Mr and Mrs Lindsey. By 1783 the congregation's further expansion necessitated the appointment of an associate minister, to allow Lindsey more time for his writing. Today, Essex Street is the site of the British Unitarian Headquarters. The chapel no longer exists, however, having been bombed in the Second World War.

While Lindsey's ministry was centred on London, Priestley was particularly important for his work in Birmingham, where he was minister of the New Meeting House, as well as a member of the Lunar Society, a group of scientists who met regularly to discuss their scientific research. Priestley was also a political activist, and a supporter of the ideals of the French Revolution. On the night of 14 July 1791 he returned home to find his house ablaze: a crowd of demonstrators mistakenly assumed that he was one of the organizers of an event commemorating the Fall of the Bastille. Priestley was obliged to escape to London, where he found refuge in Lindsey's home. He took charge of the Gravel Pit Chapel in Hackney for a short time, but in 1794 he resigned, to set off for New York. Priestley preferred the republican government of the United States, and set out in the hope of aiding the anti-slavery movement there.

Thomas Belsham – the third member of the trio – was the son of an Independent minister. Belsham taught biblical studies at Daventry where, although still a Trinitarian, he encouraged his students to examine as wide a variety of ways of interpreting the Bible as possible, whether they were Trinitarian, Arian or Socinian. At first, Belsham was disappointed at various students opting for Unitarian interpretations of scripture in preference to Trinitarian ones, but as he examined various texts and competing explanations he gradually became drawn to the Unitarian accounts. He believed that he could no longer teach biblical studies in Daventry, and consequently resigned his position. He came to London where he became Professor of Divinity and resident tutor at Hackney College. Unitarianism was acceptable there: Priestley himself was a lecturer in history and philosophy.

Belsham became minister of the Essex Street Chapel in 1805. He is said to have enjoyed poor health, being exceptionally obese: it is rumoured that the stairway leading to his pulpit had to be widened to enable him to get up to preach! In his later years he became unable to walk without the use of crutches. Belsham was one of the first members of the clergy to reject the biblical account of the six-day creation, believing it to be irreconcilable with Darwin's evolutionary theory, and he was one of the earliest exponents of the 'multiple authorship' theory of the Pentateuch (the first five books of the Judaeo-Christian Bible), previously held to have been dictated by God to Moses.

THE SEAT OF AUTHORITY

In Joseph Priestley and Thomas Belsham we can, in hindsight, see a tension between trusting one's reason to lead where it will, and trusting the Bible as the ultimate authority on religious truth. On the one hand Priestley sought to show that his doctrines of the person of Christ ('Christology') and of the Trinity were founded in scripture, but on the other hand he was distrustful of the myths surrounding Jesus' birth, and of the outmoded biblical world view which included demons and exorcisms. Priestley, however, rationalist though he was, did not reject miracles outright: indeed, he believed Jesus' performance of powerful miracles was a sign of his special authority and 'chosenness' by God. Priestley never directly addressed the question of what one should choose if reason were found to contradict scripture.

Until the 19th century the question never explicitly arose. Until the German Protestant scholars began to call into question the inerrancy which had previously been ascribed to the Bible, it had been assumed that the Bible was the linchpin of the Christian faith, and that the task of men and women was to interpret it. As science and biblical scholarship progressed, parts of the Bible became more problematical. For example, Lyell's discovery of fossils which appeared to be millions of years old was hard to reconcile with a creation which – according to James Ussher (1581–1656), a former Archbishop of Armagh – occurred in 4004 BCE. (Ussher was extremely precise in his dating of the beginning of creation, even specifying a date and time – 22 October, at 6pm!) Darwin's account of the evolution of species called into question the notion that humanity was created as a distinctive species, the pinnacle of God's creation. Biblical scholarship suggested that the five Books of Moses were probably not written by one man, transcribing his special revelation on Mount Sinai, but were edited collections of accounts by various writers, probably emanating from different backgrounds and periods of time. Parts of the Bible seemed to contradict each other, while other parts – such as the miracle stories – seemed less than credible to minds which were becoming increasingly influenced by developments in science. Indeed the period of the Enlightenment (from the 18th century onwards) caused men and women to be thrown back to the canon of reason to determine what was or was not true: in the light of the developing sciences, it seemed reasonable to believe in a universe which consistently obeyed scientific laws; it seemed less reasonable to believe in a universe whose regularities could be violently interrupted or overturned by the whim of an intervening – perhaps interfering – deity.

It was James Martineau (1805–1900), the celebrated Unitarian scholar, who marked a watershed in the development of Unitarian thought by addressing head on the problem of possible conflicts between reason and scripture. Martineau wrote a highly influential work entitled *The Seat of Authority in Religion*, in which he argued that one should no longer regard the Bible as a supreme authority to be interpreted through human reason. Martineau's important work is a lengthy study of the various sources of authority on which the Church typically relied: the authority of the Church's tradition, the authority of scripture and the authority of Jesus himself. Martineau's conclusion was that the only true sources of authority were reason and conscience and that these were the touchstones for determining how much reliance should be placed on any other supposed authority. Not only were there genuine conflicts between reason and scripture but, where such conflicts arose, the touchstone was no longer to be blind faith in scripture, but rather in reason, which was God given and, if used aright, to be trusted in determining matters of religious truth.

Unitarians today would follow Martineau here: reason is the final arbiter of truth, not faith, whether that faith be in a person, a church, or a set of scriptures. Martineau had acknowledged that the discovery of religious truth could no longer be regarded as a result of reason and scripture working in tandem: there were genuine conflicts between the two, and where such conflicts were apparent, reason should prevail. After all, as the scholarship of his time was revealing, the scriptures themselves were the result of human reason and experience, not divine dictation.

Had it not been for Martineau, it is possible that Unitarianism might have remained a Christian group, which drew its inspiration solely from scripture, and studied it through the eyes of faith – although obviously their interpretations of scripture would have remained radically different from those of other Christians.

Unitarianism Becomes a Denomination

With Theophilus Lindsey we see the first founding of an explicitly Unitarian church. As other congregations, principally from the Presbyterians and from the Baptists, became Unitarian, a need for greater organization became apparent. In 1806 a Unitarian Fund was set up to advance the Unitarian cause, and Richard Wright (1764–1836) became the first itinerant missionary. Wright was particularly important for his work in east Lancashire, where he was able to bring in the 'Cookites', followers of Joseph Cook, a Methodist minister in Rochdale, who had been expelled for heresy in the same year.

Wright also travelled in Scotland and Wales. In Wales Unitarianism proved particularly popular, so much so that Cardiganshire became known as the 'Black Spot'. This name refers to the appearance of the area when Unitarian congregations are marked on the map: the area is a mass of black dots! As well as Wright's influence, the Rev David Davis of Llwynrhydowen did much to propagate radicalism from his prestigious school at Castle Howell Farm. Although he did not call himself a Unitarian, he is justly regarded as the father of Welsh Unitarianism.

In 1825 the British and Foreign Unitarian Association was formed, to oversee denominational affairs in England, Wales and Scotland. Martineau, however, wanted a wider, more ecumenical, Christian organization, and founded the 'National Conference of Unitarian, Liberal Christian, Free Christian, Presbyterian and other Non-Subscribing or Kindred Congregations' – a somewhat daunting name! In a small denomination, it seemed undesirable to have two overseeing organizations, and in 1928 the General Assembly of Unitarian and Free Christian Churches emerged. This is the organization to which all British Unitarians belong today.

The situation in Ireland is somewhat different. The Non-Subscribing Presbyterian Church of Ireland (NSPCI) was formed in 1910, uniting the Presbytery of Antrim (founded 1725) and the Remonstrant Synod (founded 1829), both of which found problems in subscribing to the Westminster Confession of Faith of 1647. The non-subscribers tended to be Arian (they viewed Jesus Christ as more than human, but less than God), hence they have tended to be more conservative and more overtly Christian in ethos than Unitarians in England, Scotland and Wales. Many NSPCI members today consider themselves Unitarians and, like the Unitarians, impose no credal tests on their members. They are permitted to attend the Unitarian General Assembly, and to vote in its affairs.

2 · UNITARIANISM IN AMERICA

The origins of Unitarianism in America can be traced back to the Great Awakening of the mid-18th century. The Age of Enlightenment had created an emphasis on reason, leading to forms of religion that lacked exuberance, without undue reliance on the emotions, preferring liturgical formalism to spontaneity. The Great Awakening was a reaction against the Enlightenment, attempting to bring back the faith and zeal that characterized evangelical Christianity.

The most prominent protagonist of the Great Awakening was Jonathan Edwards (1703–58), who started his career as a tutor at Yale University but, having undergone a conversion experience at the age of 18, devoted his life to itinerant preaching in the open air. Before his conversion, Edwards had described predestination – the Calvinist theory that God foreknows and forewills the elect and the damned – as a 'horrible doctrine'. Having become converted to a form of Protestant Calvinism, Edwards then saw the doctrine as providing a powerful assurance of God's sovereignty over everything.

George Whitefield (1714–70), who helped Edwards to spearhead this Great Awakening, was also much influenced by Calvin. He had come from England, where he had learned from John Wesley how to evangelize crowds in the open air.

The Great Awakening had a profound effect on the Dutch Reformed Church, Congregationalists, Presbyterians and Baptists but, since it was conducted largely outside, was also able to reach those who were 'unchurched'. Some of its supporters extended its sights to reach the American Indians.

The message of the Great Awakening was a form of evangelical Calvinism. It emphasized faith and grace, rather than works, placing emphasis on personal commitment to newness of birth. While it did much to strengthen the commitment of some of the mainstream Protestant Churches, it met with opposition from the theological liberals. They took issue on a number of crucial points: original sin, election, individual responsibility, the traditional view of the atonement, the interpretation of scripture and biblical scholarship. When the evolutionists came to the fore, Darwinism also became an issue which divided the orthodox and liberal camps. Whitefield brought his mission to Boston, Massachusetts but, although he secured substantial support, he also succeeded in alienating many from his brand of religion.

Among his earliest opponents was the Rev Ebenezer Gay (1696–1787), minister at Hingham, a position which he occupied for no less than 68 years. Gay has the distinction of being one of the first American clergy to deny the doctrine of the Trinity, and for this reason he is sometimes known as the 'father of American Unitarianism'. Other opposition, on somewhat different grounds, came from Charles Chauncy (1705–87), who was ordained in Boston's First Church in 1727. Chauncy could not accept that God would eternally condemn anyone to hell, let alone predestine individuals to everlasting punishment. By contrast, he advocated a doctrine of universal salvation. Chauncy wrote a treatise entitled *The Mystery Hid from Ages and Generations* which he completed in the 1750s and circulated to sympathizers. However, it was not finally published until 1784.

Another significant milestone in Unitarianism's development occurred in 1785. The King's Chapel in Boston, which was Episcopalian, had no minister to lead the congregation, and James Freeman, a ministerial student, was invited to act as Reader and subsequently Pastor. Like Gay, Freeman had problems about the Trinity, and confided them to his congregation, who were sympathetic. Freeman was allowed to modify the words of the Prayer Book, expunging Trinitarian references, and to omit the recitation of the Athanasian and Nicene Creeds from the liturgy. The congregation thus became the first Unitarian church in America. Two years later the question arose as to whether Freeman might become formally ordained. The Episcopalian Church declined to give an immediate reply, and so the congregation took it upon themselves to conduct Freeman's ordination, thus precipitating a separation from the Episcopalians.

Things came to a head in 1805, when Henry Ware (1764-1845), who was known for his liberal opinions, was appointed as the Hollis Professor of Divinity at Harvard, in succession to a Calvinist. This was the oldest endowed chair in the university, and hence highly prestigious. The appointment, understandably, did not please the conservatives (Calvinists). Two Calvinists in particular – Jedediah Morse and Jeremiah Evans – produced pamphlets which scorned the liberals and deplored their theology. 'Shall we have the Boston religion, or the Christian religion?' Morse asked provocatively.

PRIESTLEY ARRIVES

When Joseph Priestley arrived from England in 1794 he had hoped to find a more tolerant environment in which he could continue his scientific and philosophical study. Very soon after his arrival, however, he was persuaded to lecture on religion in Philadelphia, where in 1796 he established 'the first permanent Unitarian church in America'.[1]

Priestley attached particular importance to Christology, claiming that Christianity had tended to elevate Christ to an unwarrantedly high status, first as a divine being, equal with God, and then as the second member of the Holy Trinity.

Priestley affirmed 'the simple humanity of Christ' regarding him as nothing more than a 'mere man', although one who was aided by God. Priestley's position, in common with Lindsey and Belsham back in England, was more radical than the American liberals, who have often been labelled 'Arians'. The name 'Arian' is derived from the ancient heretic Arius (c250–336), who held that Christ was 'of like substance with the Father' and not 'of one substance' with him; Arius also denied the 'eternal pre-existence' of Christ, claiming that, since he was God's son, and since sons come after fathers, there must have been 'a time when he was not'. All this may sound rather technical and hair-splitting, but throughout their history Christians have been sensitive to such distinctions. For our present purposes, the point is that, although most of the American Unitarians denied the strict deity of Christ, they were still prepared – unlike Priestley – to ascribe to him a divine (or at least semi-divine) status.

The distinction between Arianism and Socinianism (Priestley's position – a supporter of Faustus Socinus, who viewed Jesus as purely human) was one which the American liberals were keen to maintain. When Thomas Belsham's *Memoirs of Theophilus Lindsey* (1812) was published in Britain, Jedediah Morse – a vociferous opponent of the liberals – reprinted a chapter which was devoted to American Unitarianism, and attempted to use this as evidence that American and British Unitarian views of Jesus Christ were identical. Morse accused them of dishonesty, claiming that they did not proclaim their views on Christ publicly from the pulpit, but circulated them secretly. The liberals, he contended, ought formally to separate from the orthodox camp.

WILLIAM ELLERY CHANNING (1780–1842)

William Ellery Channing had emerged as the leader of the liberals, and was able to reply to Morse. Channing insisted that his position did not entail that Jesus was merely human, and that he was unhappy with the label 'Unitarian', a name which had been imposed by others. The liberals preferred to be known as Liberal, Rational or Catholic Christians. He did not preach the Trinity from the pulpit because, he believed, it was unproductive to do so, and needlessly contentious.

Channing is best known for his famous sermon, 'Unitarian Christianity' (1819), which has been described as the 'Pentecost of American Unitarianism'. It was 90 minutes long, and contained a sustained attack on the Calvinists. Channing argued that Calvinism was unreasonable, untrue to the Bible and pessimistic. More positively, Channing stated in this sermon that the Bible contained successive revelations, not all of which were equally important. The New Testament was preferable to the Old, and Jesus' teachings were to be rated the highest. Scripture had to be harmonized with God's will and with the laws of nature. The meaning of the Bible had to be established in the same way as one would interpret all other books.

One criticism to which the liberals were sensitive was that they had only a lukewarm commitment to religion, and that they were not as 'pious' as their Calvinist counterparts. In 1826 Channing preached another momentous sermon entitled 'Unitarian Christianity most Favorable to Piety'. Channing chose nine key Christian doctrines, and compared the Calvinist and the liberal positions, contending – perhaps predictably – that Unitarian piety was superior. In this sermon Channing criticized the Calvinist doctrine of atonement, saying that Jesus' death at Calvary was like a gallows set up at the centre of the universe for a public hanging of an innocent victim. Needless to say, the Calvinists were outraged, but the Unitarians were delighted.

As controversy grew, it became increasingly apparent that the two religious camps could not co-exist. Particular problems arose when a pulpit became vacant. In Massachusetts the usual method of electing a new minister was at parish level, where only the men were entitled to vote. By contrast, the church itself was a smaller body, consisting mainly of women, who subscribed to the church's declaration of faith and received the sacrament regularly. As a consequence, the parish vote did not always reflect the prevalent feeling of the majority of the congregation who attended worship. In 1818 the First Church in Dedham had a vacant pulpit; the male parishioners voted in a liberal, whereas the congregation expressed a preference for a conservative. The majority party in the congregation took themselves off with much of the church's property and formed their own schismatical Church. The minority party took the case to court to recover their property, only to find – much to their astonishment – that they lost. The parish was held to be the final authority on the appointment of ministers. The conservatives accused the judge of bias, since he was in fact a Unitarian!

The result of the Dedham case favoured the liberals, but on other occasions the conservatives found that this precedent counted in their favour. Some churches went to the liberals and others to the conservatives. By 1820 the Unitarian clergy were beginning to band themselves formally together, and in 1825 the American Unitarian Association was established.

THE RISE OF BIBLICAL CRITICISM

Until around this time, both the conservative and the liberal camps in the 19th century agreed that the Bible was the authoritative scripture and a source of revelation of God's plan of salvation. However, a cluster of related issues divided the two parties. The conservatives held that the Bible was inerrant, and that it was equally inspired throughout. Although they conceded that each part was not equally clear, they subscribed to Calvin's principle that unclear and apparently ambiguous passages were to be understood in the light of those that were clearer. In other words, the Bible was its own interpreter. Further, Calvin's supporters held that the Bible supported the tenets of the creeds: the deity of Christ, the Trinity, the concept of original sin, the doctrine of election and predestination, and the traditional theories of atonement, were all to be found within scripture.

The liberal camp increasingly came to find difficulty with all these points. Although they accepted the authority of scripture, the most significant division emerged over how the Bible was to be interpreted. While agreeing that scripture contained God's revelation to humanity, they argued that human reason was nevertheless needed in order to interpret it correctly. The late 18th and early 19th centuries had seen the rise of critical biblical scholarship, and news of the work carried out by British scholars had begun to cross the Atlantic. In order to understand the Bible, the liberals contended, one must treat it as critically as any other piece of secular writing. Textual criticism was needed to establish a correct reading of the text, and a historical approach had to be taken to ascertain the extent of the Bible's reliability as a record of past events.

One young scholar whose work was particularly influential in this regard was Joseph Stevens Buckminster (1784–1812). During his short life span (he died aged 28) he did a remarkable amount to shape the future thinking of Unitarians. Buckminster was one of the first scholars to become acquainted with German contributions to biblical criticism, which were much more radical than those being made in Britain. Buckminster's studies of the Bible led him to conclude that the Bible itself should not be regarded as an inspired book, but rather as a collection of writings by inspired people. Just as humans vary in their degrees of inspiration, he claimed, so do the authors of the Bible: the writers of the gospels, for example, were more at the heart of the Christian faith than Paul or the authors of the (so-called) Old Testament. In making such a claim, Buckminster was challenging the unity of scripture.

Like his predecessors, Buckminister questioned whether several of the doctrines of the creed were truly anchored in scripture, in particular the doctrine of the Trinity.

THE TRANSCENDENTALIST CONTROVERSY

The view that scripture was the final authority had been questioned within Unitarian circles from a number of fronts. Among the groups spearheading a departure from the more Bible-based Unitarian position were the 'Transcendentalists',

such as Ralph Waldo Emerson (1803–82) and Theodore
Parker (1810–60). Chapter 8 explores Emerson's influence in
greater detail.) The rationalists were a reacting against Locke,
who regarded knowledge as coming through the senses; the
Transcendentalists set greater store on the (presumed) faculty
of intuition, by means of which religious truth could be
discerned.

According to the Transcendentalists, religious truth was
not to be found within the formal confines of a book such as
the Bible, or a church. God could be found in the whole
of nature. A claim of this kind, of course, took the
Transcendentalists away from Bible-centred, or even church-
centred religion. Parker distinguished between 'The Transient
and the Permanent in Christianity', the title of a famous
sermon which he preached on 19 May 1841 at South Boston.
In this sermon, Parker not only consigned the creeds
and the doctrine of the Trinity to the realm of humanly
devised ephemera; even the church itself was part of the
'transient'. All that remained as the 'permanent' was
'absolute, pure morality; absolute, pure religion; the love
of man; the love of God acting without let or hindrance.
The only creed it lays down is the great truth which
springs up spontaneously in the holy heart that there is
a God'.[2]

For expressing such radical views Parker became very
unpopular with his fellow clergy, many of whom completely
ostracized him. Others tried to persuade him to resign his
ministry. Parker, however, believed that religious freedom
should prevail, and refused to do so. The controversy
surrounding Parker's sermon, in fact, is the nearest that
Unitarians have ever come to conducting a heresy trial, or
formulating a set of beliefs that might serve as a precondition
for membership. In 1850, the AUA (American Unitarian
Association) unanimously adopted a motion which stated:

> Resolved, That the divine authority of the Gospel, as founded
> on a special and miraculous interposition of God for the
> redemption of mankind, is the basis of the action of this
> Association.[3]

This resolution may have reassured the more conservative Unitarians, but it made little difference to the presence of the radicals.

THE FREE RELIGIOUS ASSOCIATION

Eventually, it became clear that the real split between the conservative Christians and the Unitarians was not so much on their views of the person of Christ, but on the issue of whether creedal tests were appropriate or whether religious freedom was to prevail. Unitarian leaders like Henry Bellows (1814–82) and James Freeman Clarke (1810–88) had hoped to see a 'broad church' which would encompass a wide range of views, while being basically Christian in character.

However, Bellows and Clarke had their opponents who did not wish to assume a Christian identity, preferring the description 'Unitarian' to 'Christian'. The Rev Octavius Brooks Frothingham (1822–95) was one Unitarian minister who renounced the term 'Christian', and felt that the denomination had tended to propagate the view that its members were 'disciples of the Lord Jesus Christ', aiming to establish his kingdom on earth. Together with a number of like-minded ministers, Frothingham established the Free Religious Association, whose declared aim was 'to promote the interests of pure religion, to encourage the scientific study of theology, and to increase fellowship in the spirit'.[4]

When one leading Unitarian suggested that those 'who have ceased to accept Jesus as pre-eminently their spiritual leader and teacher' should leave the Unitarian fold, Frothingham expressed surprise that his name continued to appear in the 1873 Unitarian Year Book. He requested its removal, whereupon a number of other Unitarian ministers were placed under scrutiny and removed. Predictably, the more conservative Unitarians were pleased, and the radicals outraged. It took 10 years of heated debate before the ministers were finally reinstated.

So far, the main points of disagreement amongst Unitarians had centred on the status of Jesus. But what about God? If a denomination allowed unlimited religious freedom, did not this mean that atheists and agnostics might also be accepted within the Unitarian fold? The issue was debated at the Ministerial Conference at Cincinnati in 1886, although at that time it was largely a hypothetical problem. After hearing arguments on both sides, the Conference agreed by a substantial majority 'that the Western Unitarian Conference conditions its fellowship on no dogmatic tests, but welcomes all who wish to join it to help establish Truth and Righteousness and Love in the World'.[5]

UNIVERSALISM

Thus far I have spoken about 'Unitarians' in the USA. As a description of the present-day denomination, however, this is not strictly accurate. Following a merger with the Universalists in 1961, the national organization is called the 'Unitarian Universalist Association' (UUA), and individual members are referred to as Unitarian Universalists, or 'UUs' for short.

Something must be said about Universalism, and its legacy to present-day UUs. The Universalists, as their name implies, believed in universal salvation: they found it inconceivable that a benevolent God should punish people eternally for their sins, for no obvious purpose. A benevolent God must surely will that all people should be saved, and, being omnipotent, he must have the power to bring this about.

America's 'father of Universalism' was a preacher called John Murray (1741–1815), who started his career in Gloucester in England. Persecuted for his teachings in England, Murray decided to seek his fortune on the other side of the Atlantic, and departed by boat in 1770. His boat was grounded at New Jersey, where by chance he encountered a wealthy farmer called Thomas Potter. Potter had commissioned a chapel to be built on his property, to which he invited itinerant preachers, in the hope that one day he would hear a message that he would find amenable. Murray was invited to preach while his boat was still aground, and the sermon he preached to Potter and his neighbours was on the theme of universal grace. This was the message Potter had been waiting for.

Having converted Potter to Universalism, Murray continued to New York, and then to the colonies. In 1774, he went to Gloucester, Massachussetts, where, together with Winthrop Sargent, a ship's captain, he founded the Universalist Church in 1779.

It should be obvious that the Universalists had much in common with the Unitarians. The famous American Unitarian, Thomas Starr King (1824–64), said that the difference between Unitarians and Universalists was that the Universalists thought that God was too good to condemn humankind to be damned for ever, whereas the Unitarians thought that humankind was too good to be damned!⁸

In this respect at least, it may look as if Unitarians and Universalists were reaching similar conclusions in different ways. However, in the 19th century there remained several important differences which really made the possibility of union much less realistic than it later proved to be. First, Universalists acquired the reputation of being somewhat more rough and ready than the Unitarians. Unitarians stressed rigorous training for their clergy, and high standards of scholarship. By contrast, a significant number of Universalist clergy had been self-appointed itinerant preachers, who had previously followed a trade. Hosea Ballou (1771–1852), for example, was self-educated, and received ordination when Elhanan Winchester, founder of the Universalist Church in London in 1793, decided, at the climax of his sermon one Sunday, to press a Bible on his chest and declare him ordained on the spot!

Perhaps more significantly, the Universalists were theologically more conservative than the Unitarians. They believed in the authority of scripture; indeed, towards the end of the 19th century, they declared that they would subscribe to 'no doctrine not clearly taught in the Bible'. They were more inclined than the Unitarians to give Jesus a central position, often ascribing to him a role which far exceeded the view of the Unitarians like Priestley that he was a 'mere man', no less human or more divine than any other human being, and that his central work was as a teacher and an example to follow. Although by no means agreed on their Christology, Universalists often viewed Jesus as a divine being, even as a member of the Trinity, and they typically saw Jesus as God's messiah who served as an atoning sacrifice on the cross.

The Universalists had a creed in the form of the Winchester Profession of Belief (1803), which affirmed belief in the revelation of scriptures, the oneness of God who revealed himself through Christ and the Holy Spirit, and the importance of good works. Even though many who belonged to the Unitarian camp might well have been capable of affirming the points of the Winchester Profession, Unitarians have consistently avoided attempts to impose doctrinal tests on their members.

It may be worth mentioning that the Universalists themselves had their own internal disagreements. If one accepts the premise that all men and women will be saved, and none will be consigned to eternal damnation, it does not follow that there will be no suffering after death. Some Universalists held the view that, because of sin, most, if not all, human beings would not be ready to enter into the perfection of God's kingdom, but would require some period of purification, which might vary according to one's deeds. These Universalists became known as 'Restorationists', since they believed that humanity still had to be restored, even after death. By contrast, the 'ultra-Universalists', as they were sometimes called, claimed that there was no further suffering after death, and that, whatever one's misdeeds, one could still expect to attain everlasting life.

Feelings ran high over this controversy. In 1798, John Murray invited Hosea Ballou to take over his pulpit for several Sundays, while he went south on one of his itinerant missions. One Sunday, after Ballou had preached, John Murray's wife Judith interrupted the service to declare that, 'the doctrine which has been preached here this afternoon is not the doctrine which is usually preached in this house'.[7]

Such controversies proved to be of little interest to the Unitarians, who tended to regard ultra-Universalism in particular as morally dangerous, since it suggested that, however evil one's deeds, one could still be assured of eternal happiness. Good works, rather than reliance on divine grace, were of supreme importance to Unitarians.

In the 20th century, the common elements between Unitarians and Universalists came to outweigh past differences. After the Second World War, negotiations began to bring the two denominations together, and a merger was successfully achieved in 1961, when the Unitarian Universalist Association (UUA) was formed.

It is perhaps worth mentioning that, although Canadian Unitarians and Universalists were involved in the 1961 merger, Canadians simply refer to themselves as Unitarian rather than UU. (Canadian Unitarians have a separate distinctive identity in the Canadian Unitarian Council (CUC).) There were considerably fewer Universalist churches in Canada before the merger, and all agreed to assume a less cumbersome title, even though this meant dropping the word 'Universalist'. In Britain, no question of any such merger ever arose. Although many mainstream Christians have in fact moved towards a universalist theological position, the last British Universalist churches died out in the early part of the 20th century.

3 · WHO ARE THE UNITARIANS?

Those who define Unitarians as 'the ones that deny the Trinity' are probably thinking of the denomination's historical origins, which I explored in previous chapters. However, debates about the Trinity, the independent existence of the Holy Spirit, the non-adoration of Jesus Christ, the nature of the sacraments, and the authority of scripture, are not issues that loom large amongst present-day Unitarians. It is important to remember that members are called 'Unitarians', not 'Anti-Trinitarians'! We must therefore look to the present as well as to the past to discover what Unitarianism means.

In his recent book, *The Unitarian Path*, Andrew Hill offers the following definition of Unitarianism:

> The Unitarian path is a liberal religious movement rooted in the Jewish and Christian traditions but open to insights from world faiths, reason and science; and with a spectrum extending from liberal Christianity through to religious humanism.[1]

It should be noted that Hill uses the word 'spectrum', with good reason. Because of the diversity of Unitarian thought, different members will give widely varying accounts of what Unitarianism is and what it means to them. I offer but one.

Hill rightly draws attention to Unitarianism's roots in the Judaeo-Christian tradition. According to Calvin and his followers, God created the world and placed a man and a woman in it with the instruction not to eat of a certain tree (the tree of life) in the Garden of Eden. When Adam and Eve disobeyed God, they fell from grace; their sin not only caused them to be evicted from their idyllic paradise, but also affected all subsequent generations of humanity, who became tainted with sin, even before they were born. These ideas constitute the doctrine of the Fall and the doctrine of original sin. Ever since then humanity has been unable to pull itself up by its own boot straps. Salvation can only come through grace, and even if we engage in good deeds, 'all our righteous acts are like filthy rags' in God's sight (Isaiah 64.6). The literal meaning of the word 'grace' is 'undeserved favour', and if grace is undeserved then all attempts to deserve it are in vain. In order to be saved then the aspirant can only wait to see if he or she will become the unworthy recipient of divine favour. All comes from God, nothing from humanity. As the Westminster Confession of Faith, which was heavily influenced by Calvinism, put it:

> Works done by unregenerate men, although, for the matter of them, they may be things which God commands, and of good use both to themselves and others; yet, because they proceed not from an heart purified by faith; nor are done in a right manner, according to the word; nor to a right end, the glory of God; they are therefore sinful, and cannot please God, or make a man meet to receive grace from God. And yet their neglect of them is more sinful, and displeasing unto God.[2]

('Men', incidentally, in the above quotation, includes 'women'!) For Calvin, the notion of divine grace entailed that God selected those who are to be saved, through his divine volition alone, and – for reasons known only to himself – rejected others from his kingdom, consigning them eternally to outer darkness. This doctrine is known as 'double predestination', meaning that from the moment of creation

God, being all-powerful and all-knowing, could see in advance who would belong to the 'elect' and who would not. Being all-powerful, God must have been able to change things if he had so wished, and hence his decision to elect some and to damn others must be in accordance with his will, and somehow (although Calvin conceded that he did not know how) must be compatible with his love, mercy and justice.

Because men and women were incapable of redeeming themselves through their own efforts, those whom God planned to save had to be saved through divine grace – the sending of Jesus Christ, who was both God and man, to die on the cross for the sins of the world. Jesus' death thus atoned for human sin, and endowed those whom God chose to partake in his kingdom.

That, I suppose, is one way of interpreting the story of humankind's Fall and subsequent redemption. Yet, despite the spectrum of views which co-exist amongst Unitarians, I doubt if any could endorse this somewhat dismal Calvinist view of human nature. There is another way of understanding the biblical story, which Unitarians would favour, and it is this.

First of all, Unitarians would view the stories of the world's creation and of Adam and Eve as myth – a pictorial way of identifying humanity's position in the world – rather than as a literal attempt to write ancient history. According to the creation myth, when God created the world, he surveyed his handiwork: 'God saw all that he had made, and it was very good' (Genesis 1.31). By this time, God had already created Adam and Eve, and hence they too were part of his perfect creation. While many mainstream Christians affirm the doctrinal of original sin, Unitarians are more likely to point to a notion of 'original virtue' which is implicit in this story: Adam and Eve are not be understood as 'totally depraved', but as having the potential for good, and in the same way men and women today have the propensity for good as well as evil.

This being so, Unitarians have not emphasized the need for grace to anything like the same extent as the Calvinists. Jesus was therefore not an atoning sacrifice, either to appease a wrathful god who demanded a blood offering as an atonement for sin, or to pay some ransom to Satan who was holding humankind against its will. Jesus, in common with numerous other prophets and religious leaders, was an example to follow and a teacher with a profound message about how to live one's life. For Unitarians it is the teaching *of* Jesus that has profound significance, not the teaching *about* Jesus. Men and women have sufficient good within themselves to be able to hear an ethic of love and justice and to put it into practice.

Because Unitarians have taught that men and women have essential goodness within themselves, they have consistently rejected notions of eternal punishment. Not even the most evil members of the human race deserve eternal torment, a punishment which appears to serve no ultimate purpose and which – being never-ending – would grossly exceed the pain and suffering which even people like Jack the Ripper, Adolf Hitler or Pol Pot have ever inflicted on others. It seems all the more difficult to reconcile the notion of an all-loving God with the notion that this God has deliberately created 'vessels fitted for destruction' – people whom he has planned to punish eternally. Whatever the spectrum of beliefs in an after-life – a theme to which we shall return later – it would be fair to say that few, if any, Unitarians have sympathy with notions of eternal punishment and predestination.

WHAT ABOUT JESUS AND THE HOLY SPIRIT?

Not only have Unitarians typically questioned the Calvinist view of humanity's predicament, but they have found it incomprehensible that the action of one man – Jesus of Nazareth – dying on a cross in Jerusalem in or around the year CE 33, could somehow transform this evil race of people into redeemed men and women, who suddenly became 'justified' (made righteous) in God's sight.

Despite their problems with traditional theories of atonement, Unitarians have a high regard for Jesus. All would see him as a great teacher, and some would go so far as to say that he was the greatest religious teacher of all time. Most Unitarians would be sceptical about the gospels' portrayal of Jesus as a miracle worker, preferring to see him as a truly human figure, who offers a more realistic example to follow. Since most human beings cannot perform miracles, they can scarcely follow the model of someone who supposedly can!

Most Unitarians would see Jesus as a 'man of his time', to use a popular cliché. His life and teachings do not offer instant solutions to all life's problems. Few, if any, would have sympathy with the evangelical preacher who taught me, when I was younger, that any moral dilemma was resolved by asking, 'What would Jesus have done?' The gospel writers give us far too little information to enable us to answer such a question, and we cannot know what a first century Jewish rabbi would have done 2,000 years later in a radically different society. Would he have voted Labour or Tory, Democratic or Republican? Would he have joined the Campaign for Nuclear Disarmament? Would he have aided the plot to assassinate Hitler in the Second World War? Would he have advocated abortion and euthanasia?

Many Unitarians would prefer to admit that there is no easy way to resolve such problems, and that they must use their own reason and conscience to reach a decision when one is needed. While Jesus may influence their thinking, their ideas might also be shaped by others who have helped to guide humanity's thoughts on such areas. This might include the leading figures of the world's religious traditions, but also less renowned people, such as authors and journalists, who have contributed to these debates.

This last point leads on to a Unitarian view of the Holy Spirit. In his gospel, John tells how Jesus promised that God's Spirit would come on them after his death, and that they would be inspired and guided into all truth. Some Christians in recent times have taken this to refer specifically to Pentecost when the Holy Spirit is said to have descended on the disciples in 'tongues of fire', enabling them to 'speak in tongues'. In Pentecostalist churches, this phenomenon – 'glossolaliation', to give it its technical name – is emphasized, and great importance placed on a somewhat unintelligible way of speaking which is taken to be the hallmark of the Spirit's inspiration.

Unitarians definitely do not speak in tongues, and would hold that any such activity lacked any point or meaning. In contrast, they would tend to see the Spirit's inspiration as something that can be possessed, in varying degrees, by anyone. God's Spirit may have inspired the writers of the Judaeo-Christian scriptures, but it also inspired the great, as well as the not quite so great, figures of other religious traditions. It continues to influence writers, poets, novelists, and ordinary men and women today. Unitarians would probably not wish to set limits on the ways in which the Spirit can inspire, although of course they might caution that not every human utterance by any means is the work of the Spirit. John said, 'Do not believe every spirit, but test the spirits to see whether they are from God' (1 John 4.1). Unitarians might well agree, claiming that reason and conscience were the final arbiters of what is true inspiration. The onus rests with each member of a Unitarian church to decide for himself or herself where the truth lies.

In Britain, Unitarians produced a package for study in congregational groups, entitled, 'Build Your Own Theology' (BYOT). This perhaps sums up where Unitarians stand. There is no set theology that is laid down, and Unitarians have tended to react badly to those religions that claim to have one final prophet with whom divine revelations are 'sealed'. Unitarians have much more affinity with the reluctant 'messiah' in the comic film *The Life of Brian*, who tried to teach people that, 'You must work things out for yourself'.

Whatever conclusions a member reaches, one thing is certain. The minister is not likely to take people aside and remind them that they are not espousing 'true doctrine' or point out any presumed discrepancies between their views and what is written in a sacred text. Unitarians must indeeed 'work things out for themselves'.

A FAITH WITHOUT A CREED?

All this may sound somewhat anarchic. When people hear of the amount of flexibility and freedom that Unitarianism affords, a commonly asked question is, 'What holds Unitarians together?' How is it possible to have a faith without a creed? If there is no creed, then what is it that Unitarians have in common?

Firstly, the idea that one needs a creed to bind a religious community together is very much a mainstream Christian notion. Throughout its history Christianity has had a preoccupation with defining itself in terms of creeds, catechisms and confessions of faith, and it has used these credal formulations to define who can remain inside the Christian fold and who must be excluded. Those who denied the full deity, or the full humanity of Jesus Christ, who claimed that there must have been a time before he came into existence, or that God the Father died on the cross, or that people are saved through works rather than faith, or that the soul reincarnates after death – all of these have, at one time or another been considered to be vicious heretics to be placed beyond the Christian pale.

Yet, although mainstream Christianity has operated in this way, it is really the only world religion that has defined itself credally. If one looks at Judaism, one recognizes that being a Jew is much more bound up with observing the Torah (the Mosaic Law). For a Buddhist, progress towards nirvana is much more to be desired than 'sound doctrine', and no monk can be expelled from a monastic community simply for holding unusual or unpopular views. For a Hindu, fulfilling one's *dharma* – one's social and religious obligations, which are partly defined by one's caste – is one's supreme task in life. This is not to say there are no credal elements in these religions: it would be strange for a practising Jew not to believe in the oneness of God, for a Hindu not to believe in the existence of the soul, or for the Buddhist not to believe that there exists a state called nirvana. However, like these religions, Unitarian beliefs tend to be minimal, and of secondary importance.

I have already suggested that typically they would present a positive view of humanity, a belief that Jesus was a man and not a god, that he was a great teacher, but that there are others too who can inspire and guide, and so on. But it is perfectly possible for a fellow Unitarian to question any – or all – of these points, and still have as much right as I to remain within the Unitarian fold. They would still have much in common, but it would not be credal.

What they would have in common would be a quest for truth in religion and morals, a quest which was not hampered by the restrictions of some external authority which imposed sanctions for 'false doctrine'. They would commonly enjoy an environment which encouraged individual seeking, and provided the means to make this possible. They would share a respect for all those who honestly sought truth for themselves, and a toleration of those whose views profoundly differed from their own. They would jointly seek to learn from the variety of sources which the religions of the world have made available, but they would not be obliged to subscribe to any one pre-determined set of answers. Their reason would guide them in matters of truth, their consciences in matters of morals. Finally, they would seek to put faith into practice, by seeking opportunities to promote love, justice and peace within their own community and in the wider world.

Some Unitarians have produced 'affirmations' rather than creeds, which are sometimes read in church or even recited by the congregation, to remind themselves of the basic principles to which most Unitarians would affirm their commitment. Here is one:

> Love is the doctrine of this church,
> The quest of truth is its sacrament,
> And service is its prayer.
> To dwell together in peace,
> To seek knowledge in freedom,
> To serve human need,
> To the end that all souls shall grow into harmony with the
> Divine –
> Thus do we covenant with each other and with God.[3]

The UUA Principles include this statement:

Unitarian Universalists Covenant to Affirm and Promote:

The inherent worth and dignity of every person
Justice, equity and compassion in human relations
Acceptance of one another and encouragement to spiritual
    growth in our congregations
A free and responsible search for truth and meaning
The right of conscience and the use of the democratic process
    within our congregations and in society at large
The goal of world community with peace, liberty and justice
    for all
Respect for the interdependent web of all existence, of which
    we are a part.[4]

Most Unitarians would probably feel at home with the majority of these points. Someone who profoundly disagreed with most, or who felt that they were an inadequate expression of religious commitment, would probably be unlikely to remain for long within a Unitarian congregation. But the decision rests entirely with the individual, who exercises his or her own reason and conscience in such matters.

4 · STRUCTURES AND ORGANIZATION

In the previous chapter, we mentioned that the Unitarian heritage has drawn on a wide variety of world religious traditions. This does not imply, however, that every Unitarian is an avid reader of Confucius, Lao Tzu, the Buddhist scriptures, and the Qur'an, as well as the Judaeo-Christian Bible. Like most followers of a religion, Unitarians are perfectly ordinary people, with varying degrees of education and breadth and interest in reading. In order to draw on these various sources of inspiration, however, it is not expected that Unitarians necessarily study them for themselves, although some do. It is sufficient that those who lead the worship and congregational activities are trained appropriately so that they can disseminate the fruits of their own study, to aid the spiritual life of a congregation.

For this reason Unitarians have a trained ministry, and most congregations have a trained leadership. This is an important respect in which Unitarians differ from the Quakers and from most independent churches, where the Reformation notion of the 'priesthood of all believers' is often carried to the (perhaps logical) conclusion that everyone is on the same footing with respect to their ability to 'give ministry' or to lead congregational worship.

Unitarians do not deny that there are many who welcome such ways of organizing worship, and that they can benefit from it. Indeed, Unitarians go so far as to hold that there are no special acts or ceremonies which are the exclusive prerogative of a separate ministry. If a lay member of a congregation is capable of preaching, leading the worship or making some contribution to it, there is absolutely no reason why he or she may not be asked to do so. There are no special rites, such as the celebration of communion, that may only be performed by the minister, as is the rule in most mainstream Christian Churches. There is no special 'magic' that is worked through a communion service or a christening that is only efficacious if a minister performs it. In practice, the minister, being the usual leader of the worship, normally performs any such ceremonies,[1] but, if a minister were unavailable, or if it seemed particularly appropriate for a lay person to be invited, there would be no objection.

This raises the question of whether it still makes sense in the late 20th and early 21st centuries to have a class of people called ministers, who are distinguished from the majority of lay people in the denomination. In Britain, Unitarian ministers are no longer 'ordained' at a special ceremony, indicating that they are not 'set apart' from other people. However, most would agree that there is much to be gained by having a highly trained group of people who can spend all their working time studying, preparing a high quality of worship, and using their pastoral skills to minister to the needs of their congregations and those outside. Training is rigorous, and quite a high proportion of applicants for ministerial training are turned back with the suggestion that their qualities might be better used in other ways. The skills, qualifications and experience of those who are accepted are assessed and, in the light of their backgrounds, the necessary training is worked out, which tends to be tailor-made to the individual.

In smaller congregations worship is led by a 'lay pastor' or a 'lay leader'. The difference between these two categories is that the lay pastor has completed some formal training within the denomination, although not quite as much as the fully-fledged minister. Lay leaders are chosen for their personal and intellectual properties; they will probably have some initial qualifications – not necessarily in religious studies or theology – which ensure their capability to lead others, and they will be expected to undertake some further formal study to enhance the qualities that they bring.

Whichever type of leadership a congregation has, the emphasis is always on ensuring a high quality of worship and preaching. Unitarians tend to favour a Sunday service that is carefully and thoughtfully prepared, even if it seems more coolly rational and less stirring than that of the evangelical preacher who may take a pride in not using any notes and on relying on the inspiration of the Spirit to see him (not so commonly her!) through the sermon.

Does this mean that Unitarian services are cold and clinical? Not necessarily: being in the Free Christian tradition, and hence not bound to use service books or missals, anything can happen at a service of worship – in theory at least. During my time as a Unitarian I have seen worship consist of a video followed by a discussion, a Buddhist monk guiding the congregation through a Buddhist meditation, a couple sharing their own spiritual journey with other attendees, and a service at which the congregation were issued with sheets of paper and asked to draw a symbolic picture of what Unitarianism meant to them! One can probably expect to find rather more by way of variation in some American and Canadian congregations than with most British Unitarian services and – to an even greater degree – those in Eastern Europe, who stick to a fairly formal and predictable order of worship, very much in the Christian mould.

Whatever happens, the typical Unitarian service is normally well planned in advance, and it is not expected that members of a congregation will spontaneously rise to give their testimony, engage in 'chain prayer', offer a prophetic utterance, or speak in tongues, as is sometimes characteristic of the Christian evangelical revivalist meeting. Those who are more accustomed to the exuberance and spontaneity of a Pentecostalist service have sometimes criticized Unitarian

worship for being staid and even 'clinical', although it is
certainly no more so than those churches that follow a set
liturgy. Many Unitarians are only too well aware of the
problems that can be caused by those who have attempted to
stir up crowds or unduly appeal to people's emotions, and
prefer that the congregations to which they belong should
have adequate opportunity to reflect on, and even question,
what they hear.

The choice between Unitarian and other kinds of worship
need not be an exclusive one, however. It is perfectly possible
to join a Unitarian congregation without leaving one's
previous one, and in doing so one can enjoy the best of both
worlds. There are Unitarians who are simultaneously
Quakers, for example, and who commute between the two
denominations, enjoying Quaker silence and spontaneous
ministry on one occasion and Unitarian reason the next. I
have known Unitarians who have dual membership which
encompasses variously the Swedenborgian Church, the
Rosicrucians and the Church of England. Having these 'dual
religious nationalities' not only means that it is possible to fill
in any gaps which Unitarians may fail to offer: the life of the
Unitarian congregation is also enriched by having in their
midst members who can disseminate information and
enthusiasm for ideas which do not lie within the Unitarian
tradition. This can only help to broaden one's horizons and
enhance the spirit of tolerance.

UNITARIAN STRUCTURES

Unitarianism is a democratic organization, and the style of
worship, the activities and the general policies of each
individual Unitarian church are decided at congregational
level. There is no 'line management' structure or quality
assurance system which ensures standard practice
throughout the denomination. Hungary and Romania are
distinctive in having bishops: one bishop oversees
congregations in each country, but their role is a purely
advisory one, and they seek to support congregations, rather
than dictate their policies to them. (Both bishops are

currently men, but there is no objection to female bishops.) 'Freedom, reason and tolerance – the three fundamental principles of Unitarianism – entail a spirit of trust that is placed on the integrity, not only of individuals, but of individual congregations, to decide and define their own affairs without undue interference from those outside. Having said this, it is important to recognize that a Unitarian congregation is not an independent religious community, but part of a wider body, and different areas of the globe have their own General Assemblies (GAs), of which each congregation and each member is a part, and which serve to further the Unitarian cause within that area.

There are obvious advantages in having a system of General Assemblies. To give one example: if a congregation's minister resigns or retires, a national – indeed, international – institution ensures that there is an official roll from which candidates can be selected to fill the vacancy, and that, before a candidate can be placed on the roll, he or she must have undertaken appropriate training and received due accreditation for it. A church that was totally independent – for example, some evangelical Christian churches – would merely have its own community to draw on to fill any gaps in leadership, and would have the exclusive responsibility for whatever training, if any, was thought to be necessary. Since Unitarians lay great emphasis on training and intellectual integrity, a system that consisted entirely of 'home grown' leadership would be less than satisfactory, and the wider General Assembly serves to ensure that congregations can look beyond themselves for effective and well-trained ministers.

The General Assembly meets every year, and each congregation is allowed to send at least one representative. The Assembly will consider domestic matters of business, such as finance, investments, ministerial stipends and pension schemes, and – perhaps more interestingly – define its attitudes to matters of religious and social concern. Past Assemblies that I have attended have addressed matters such as prison reform, possible decriminalization of drugs, support for the United Nations' International Year for Tolerance (1995), implementing 'green' policies, and the banning of hand guns. (The 1996 General Assembly, at which this last issue was debated, was held in Glasgow, only 30 miles from Dunblane, where 16 young schoolchildren and their teacher were massacred by an insane gunman.)

The General Assembly can thus lend its weight to campaigners for the various causes on which it decides. On its own, a letter signed by the General Secretary on behalf of the Assembly may not be sufficient to sway a government on matters of national concern, but it adds momentum to causes which other denominations and pressure groups are simultaneously supporting. To give but one example, when the British GA passed its motion on hand guns, this added one more voice to a number which helped to influence Parliament's decision later in that same year to restrict hand gun ownership very severely. Unitarians know that, when they debate an issue and act as a pressure group, there are numerous other groups with similar interests that are adding their weight too.

In matters of decision-making, however, it is with the congregation that the power of decision-making rests. General Assembly decisions have no more than an advisory status, unlike a General Synod or ecumenical council, with their authority to impose their decisions on the 'lower' echelons of the ecclesiastical ladder. Since conscience has supreme importance for Unitarians in deciding what to do, it would normally be considered wrong for an external body to interfere with anything that a congregation or an individual conscientiously decides.

AN INTERNATIONAL COUNCIL

One recent development in Unitarian and UU organization is significant: the formation of the International Council of Unitarians and Universalists (ICUU) on 25 March 1995. Unitarian congregations now exist in 20 countries and in five continents, and part of the purpose in establishing an international body of this kind was to bring Unitarians together from different parts of the globe, offering mutual support and exchange of ideas.

The ICUU was designed to address a further issue. In countries where Unitarianism was not strong, the only realistic option available to congregations was to affiliate with the continental European UUA. This seemed inappropriate, and the creation of an International Council meant that these congregations could now gain recognition at global level for their Unitarian or UU identity, without the inappropriate liaisons that were necessitated in the past.

5 · WORSHIP AND RITES OF PASSAGE

How do Unitarians worship, and what might one expect to find at a typical Sunday service? Since Unitarianism's origins, at least in Britain, lie in a refusal to use the Book of Common Prayer, it should come as no surprise to learn that there is no set order of worship or mandatory service book. Each congregation will favour its own traditional practices, and worship accordingly.

In Britain one will usually – although not necessarily – find reference to the Christian tradition. Traditionally, one type of Unitarian service is modelled on the 'hymn sandwich' that has been favoured by the Free Churches: that is to say, the service comprises prayers, readings and usually a sermon, interspersed with singing. In a few, more conservative congregations, a service book is used, which is derived from the traditional Church of England morning and evening prayer, and which contains set prayers and psalms. Sometimes, a discussion, or a video – or both – may replace the sermon. In many Unitarian churches in the USA, and in a few Unitarian churches in Britain, it is possible to attend services in which there is no reference whatsoever to Jesus or

54

to Christianity. The theme of a service might be based on some social concern (such as peace or justice), or it might relate to some aspect of another religious tradition, such as Buddhism. Each congregation's practice is determined by the minister, in consultation with his or her congregation, or maybe a worship committee. In theory at least, anything can happen!

Despite wide variations in practice, one or two generalizations are possible. Most congregations would use the Judaeo-Christian scriptures at least some of the time, and in most churches in Britain (although not all) they would normally be read on most Sundays. However, since it is believed that no single religion possesses a monopoly of truth, there is a widespread practice of having at least one reading from some other piece of writing. This could be from the sacred texts of some other tradition, from the works of an eminent Unitarian thinker or some other spiritually edifying writer. Secular writings too can be used, since there are many ways in which the divine can reveal itself. One British Unitarian minister typically reads from Christian scriptures for the first lesson, and refers to the second reading – which does not come from the Bible – as 'the continuing scripture', the logic being that one's understanding of God and of humanity did not come to an end when the last word of the New Testament was penned.

For some Unitarians, the notion of prayer, as traditionally understood, presents some difficulty. Whatever status is ascribed to prayer, few – if any – Unitarians would believe that prayer was a way of bringing about some kind of miraculous divine intervention in human affairs. Human beings, not some supernatural divine agent (if such exists), must effect whatever changes are needed in the world. Prayer, then, serves as a means of expressing one's thankfulness for the benefits of living in the world, and a means of reminding oneself of one's ideals and aspirations, the ways in which the world falls short of such ideals, and of one's own role in helping the world to become a place of greater love, peace and justice. Some Unitarians prefer the idea of meditation rather than prayer, and in some congregations some form of guided meditation supersedes the more traditional prayers. It is usual in Unitarian worship for a short period of silence to be observed, so that the congregation may reflect on the ideas that the preacher has presented, or on their own lives.

RITES

In any religious organization there are special services to mark rites of passage and festivals, and Unitarianism is no exception. The most important life-cycle events are birth, marriage and death, and all these are marked within the context of the Unitarian faith.

In many mainstream denominations there is a set liturgy which must normally be followed for sacraments such as baptism to be considered 'valid'. Unitarians have a radically different approach to rites of passage: they have little room for the notion that there are special rites which, if omitted, might jeopardize one's eternal salvation, or which, if practised, have some special kind of miraculous efficacy. James Martineau wrote of the 'debasing effect of all sacramental doctrine', which, he claimed, 'turns the Divine world into a realm of magic'.[1]

BIRTH

When a baby is born, then, there is no need to secure it a place in God's kingdom and no fear that it may end up in the state of 'limbo' if unbaptized, as traditional Roman Catholicism has taught. What is more important is how members feel about key events in their lives and how their own specific individual needs can be met within a religious context.

Different children are born in different circumstances, presenting families with different emotions and different needs. Parents will feel thankful as well as proud, and will want their child to be welcomed into the community of the church. But there may be other factors that are important to recognize too. Perhaps the birth has been a difficult one; perhaps the parents have had problems in conceiving a child at all; perhaps the child is not the natural offspring of the parents; perhaps the child has a disability.

Because participants' needs are diverse, Unitarians are particularly keen to ensure that each ceremony fits the requirements of those who take part, as precisely as possible. For this reason, the main participants will be fully consulted – the parents – and they will be strongly encouraged to contribute their own ideas. It is quite common for participants to suggest or even write their own readings to make the occasion especially 'theirs'. Some parents may wish water to be used, either to symbolize purity or cleansing, or because it is traditionally the symbol by which children have been received into the church; others may express the wish to avoid using water, since it connotes quasi-magical notions associated with Christian baptism. In some congregations the term 'baptism' is still used, while others prefer to call the ceremony a 'christening' or a 'naming' ceremony.

ADMISSION

Baptism or naming does not confer membership, nor is it a prerequisite for it. Occasionally, unbaptized adults have requested a ceremony in which (perhaps) water is used, but this is in no sense an expectation. One becomes a member of a Unitarian church according to the particular custom of the congregation, and – as one might expect in Unitarian circles – there is no standard uniform practice. In most cases the would-be member will have attended the congregation's services for approximately six months, then filled in a form of application for membership, which goes to the relevant church committee for approval. There is of no course no credal test for acceptance: the applicant simply indicates sympathy with the spirit and the aims of the congregation, and from then onwards is a member with voting rights, until he or she resigns.

Some Unitarian churches have a formal ceremony of admission, where the applicant makes certain pledges of commitment to the congregation. A few congregations invite new members to stand before them and say a few words of introduction, so that the congregation begins to know them.

A small handful of congregations in Britain do not have formal membership, believing that it creates a distinction between 'us' and 'them', between the committed and the seemingly not-so-committed. In such congregations, all who attend congregational meetings are therefore equally entitled to express their views and exercise their right to vote. Such a policy no doubt has its risks, but it seeks to be inclusive.

MARRIAGE

Just as parents may have special needs, so can marriage partners. Different couples come with very different backgrounds and different needs, and – with changing societal attitudes to partnerships – will not necessarily be the young first-timers who have traditionally been joined in matrimony within mainstream churches. Increasingly, those who seek a Unitarian marriage ceremony include divorced couples, widows and widowers, those who have already been living together, those who have already been married and wish some further religious ceremony, and couples of different faiths who seek to find some common denominator.

In an increasingly multi-faith environment, Unitarian churches have sometimes provided a solution for couples who need to find a religious building where a legally binding marriage can be solemnized, where family and guests from both cultural backgrounds will readily attend, and where neither party will be obliged to make impossible promises or be committed to unacceptable religious ideas. Although it would be an exaggeration to claim that Unitarian multi-faith marriages are common, the 'tailor made' service can enable a couple from different religious backgrounds to marry without undue compromise.

Not all marriages last 'till death us do part', of course, and some couples who are undergoing divorce wish the end of their marriage to be marked publicly, and in a religious context. After all, a divorce is just as important a milestone in one's life as one's marriage, and often friends may be reticent about mentioning the situation to those involved. Bringing one's divorce into a more public arena can be a way of removing any such taboos, and a ceremony in which both partners take part can help to remove resentments and old scores which they may subsequently try to settle.

Unitarians can offer services and ceremonies for other needs. In recent times, homosexual partners have felt a need to express publicly their commitment to each other, just as heterosexual partners have traditionally done. In Britain the practice of blessing same-sex partnerships is occasionally practised, although it is somewhat more common in the USA. Although single-sex unions have no legal status, a religious ceremony can enable the participants to express publicly their feelings with honesty and integrity and, if one may put it so, to receive a 'seal of approval' from those who attend. Most Unitarians would consider this preferable to being a 'closet homosexual'.

DEATH

In common with all other followers of religions, Unitarians have rites of passage for death. Superficially, a Unitarian funeral may not look particularly different from those of mainstream Christian denominations: there are usually readings, hymns, prayers and a tribute to the person who has died. As with child namings and weddings, Unitarians attach great importance to tailoring the service to the needs of the bereaved, making the service as personal as possible, and, in particular, attempting to meet the needs of those for whom life must continue, despite the loss. A minister or lay officiant would make a point of discussing the service thoroughly with the next of kin, to ensure that this occurs. (Many mainstream clergy adopt this practice as well.)

Since belief in life after death cannot be taken for granted, either on the part of the deceased or by the attendees, a funeral will seldom begin with Jesus' words, 'I am the resurrection and the life'. There are no absolute certainties about what lies beyond death, and Unitarians would wish to recognize this, and not offer vain assurances or false hopes.

However, despite wide differences, there is one thing on which Unitarians would tend to agree: a hell, in which the dead experience the revenge of a wrathful God, is not something which one need fear.

Unitarian funerals will tend to place greater emphasis on this world rather than the next (if it exists), celebrating the achievements of the one who has died, and providing support and encouragement to those who remain. Unlike humanist groups, Unitarians do not campaign for secular funerals, but seek to meet the needs of the religious and non-religious alike – not an easy task! The fact that most Unitarian chapels are free of Christian symbols such as crosses helps to make the environment more conducive to catering for a wide spectrum of spiritual needs.

The ideal way of achieving an appropriate funeral is for each individual to draft an outline, in advance, of their own funeral service. A number of Unitarians (including myself) have done this, and the practice is encouraged and growing. Care is needed to ensure that those who take part in such a service are allowed their own distinctive contribution, but appropriate forethought ensures that one receives an appropriate farewell. In my own case, I would particularly wish to avoid a funeral where – as commonly happens – the tribute elevated me to the status of a saint: while it might be equally inappropriate to enumerate my many shortcomings, I would at least hope for a realistic appraisal on death! Other Unitarians, no doubt, have their own particular desires, which can be met when due forethought is given.

COMMUNION

What about the 'eucharist' or Holy Communion? Unitarians are more comfortable with the term 'communion' (the adjective 'holy' is usually dropped) rather than 'eucharist' or 'mass', since 'communion' is the term which is generally used within the Non-conformist Churches. Until fairly recently British Unitarians celebrated communion as well as baptism, but, apart from the Hungarian, Transylvanian and Irish traditions, the practice of having a regular communion service is gradually dying out.

Communion commemorates the Last Supper, the final meal that Jesus shared with his disciples, according to the gospel writers. At that meal Jesus offered bread and wine to the disciples, in the style of a Jewish kiddush, and the mainstream Christian tradition has celebrated communion as a sacrament, reminding the participant that Jesus offered his body and blood as a sacrifice for humankind's sin. For Unitarians, however, communion is regarded as no more than a memorial. In common with mainstream Protestantism, Unitarians do not believe that any miraculous transformation takes place in the bread and wine, such as traditional Roman Catholics affirm in their doctrine of transubstantiation. There is no belief that in communion Jesus Christ is offered up again to God the Father as a re-enactment of the atonement on the cross, since no substitutionary sacrifice was ever needed in the first place to atone for sin. Nor is there any belief that any miraculous transformation takes place in the hearts and minds of those who receive. If there is any change, it is because of the participant's will and effort: to believe that the ritual itself had some objective power would seem nothing less than superstition.

In the Hungarian and Transylvanian tradition, communion is celebrated four times a year (Christmas, Easter, Pentecost and Harvest), and is a very solemn occasion. At the point in the service at which the elements (the bread and the wine) are distributed, the men first form a semi-circle around the table, in order of seniority. The oldest member receives the bread and wine first, and the youngest last. When the men have partaken, it is the women's turn, and the custom of receiving in order of seniority is similarly observed.

In the USA traditional communion services are rare. While respecting the views of those who see a benefit in enacting a ritual such as distributing bread and wine, most American Unitarians would regard such as ritual as having rather obscure meaning, believing that one can commemorate the life and work of Jesus by more obvious means, such as hearing the Christian message and trying to put it into practice.

In Britain, the practice varies. In most churches, communion has disappeared; where it still remains, it is celebrated in a 'low key' manner, so as not to offend those who feel that such a ritual offends one's reason. One British Unitarian church, for example, has a communion service twice a year (shortly before Christmas, and on the Thursday before Easter, the traditional anniversary of the Last Supper). This same church avoids Sunday celebrations of communion, lest it intrudes on the sensitivities of regular worshippers who might feel uncomfortable with the rite.

In modern times, the rite has been adapted for changing needs. The traditional words of institution, attributed to Jesus ('Take, eat, this is my body ... this is my blood') need not be present. In some circles, attempts have been made to change the elements which are used: occasionally Unitarian clergy have attempted to celebrate communion with cola and crisps instead of the traditional bread and wine – although it must be emphasized that this practice is not at all common! Some Unitarians might wish to reinterpret the meaning of the symbolism of communion, seeing it as a way of representing one's sense of community by symbolic food sharing, or giving thanks for the basic elements of food and drink with which they have been blessed. It may remind the participants of the value of simple things and to be thankful for them. Physical food may also serve as a reminder of the spiritual food by which one is nourished, and hence may connote the richness of wisdom to be found in Jesus' life and teaching.

One particularly striking innovation is the 'flower communion' devised by Norbert V Capek (1870–1942), a Czech Unitarian minister, and which has become increasingly popular in the USA and Europe. At the flower communion, each member comes bearing a flower, which is placed in the sanctuary area, and helps to beautify it. At the end of the service, members take a different flower and place it in their homes.

FESTIVALS

CHRISTMAS

In common with the vast majority of Westerners, Unitarians regard Christmas as a time for great celebration, for both secular and religious reasons. Like most people, they enjoy an opportunity to have festivities, to exchange presents and to sing the traditional Christmas carols; more significantly, of course, Christmas marks the birth of a great – some would say the greatest – teacher. Even if it is unlikely that Jesus of Nazareth was actually born on 25 December – the date was more probably derived from the ancient Roman Saturnalia rather than Jesus' actual birthday – that date is traditional, and Unitarians see no reason to change it.

Because of the popularity of most of the traditional carols, Christmas is the one occasion where Unitarian theology is compromised, taking second place to convention, and for once in the year Unitarians can be found singing words like, 'Hark the glad sound! the saviour comes', or, 'O come, let us adore him, Christ the Lord'.

It must be said that some Unitarians find such words something of an embarrassment, since they do not regard Jesus as the saviour or Christ. Others may suggest that they do not always agree with the words they sing in any case, and sing the Christmas hymns as the words of others, who have caused them to reflect on the meaning of Jesus' life and work. The principle of tolerance entails that Unitarians can comfortably co-exist with those mainstream Christians who can espouse more traditional views of Jesus' advent.

EASTER

Easter is the next landmark in the Christian calendar, and it is often asked what Unitarians have to celebrate on Easter morning. Unitarians have the freedom to espouse traditional Christian views of the resurrection, and, if a Unitarian finds it reasonable to believe that the stone on Jesus' tomb was miraculously rolled back and that he came back to life after being dead for over two days, then he or she can still comfortably maintain a place within a Unitarian congregation. Most Unitarians, however, being somewhat more sceptical about miracles, would wish to subject the evidence concerning the resurrection to critical scrutiny.

Many Unitarians would agree with the radical mainstream Christian scholar who stated that 'the bones of Jesus lie somewhere in Palestine'.[2] If this is so, then Unitarians certainly have a problem with Easter. The festival is not the high point of the year, as it is for mainstream Christians, but at least they can worship knowing that they are not called upon to believe in anything that stretches their credulity beyond its limits. One Unitarian congregation recently billed their Easter service as 'Easter Sunday: discussion'! One can celebrate one's doubts as well as one's certainties in Unitarian worship.

More positively, the meaning of Easter for many Unitarians is newness of life. The word 'Easter' derives from the name of the ancient Celtic goddess of spring, Eostre, whose festival was celebrated at the vernal equinox, when the trees and plants were beginning to blossom, with winter now in the past and the prospect of the warmth and fertility of summer ahead. Easter thus provides an opportunity for Unitarians to be reminded that nature itself is subject to a process of death and resurrection, and to be thankful that the plant and tree life, which has been dead in the winter, is now being revived.

Some Unitarians might see the process of death and resurrection as applying to human beings too. Just as plants and living things can be renewed, so each human soul can be revived and re-energized. If one's life has seemed dull or pointless, things can improve: the Easter themes of death and resurrection symbolize hope, and the possibility of new purpose in life.

PENTECOST

Although most Unitarian churches would mark the festivals of Christmas and Easter, it is common for Pentecost (or Whitsun) to go unmarked in congregational worship. There are no doubt several reasons for this. First, as we have seen, Unitarians never regarded the Holy Spirit as a distinct 'person' over and above God or Jesus. Second, there was no single time and place at which the Holy Spirit descended on humankind, as indeed mainstream Christianity would no doubt concede. The Bible plainly states that God's Spirit was at work at the creation of the world (Genesis 1.2), that it inspired the prophets, put life into Ezekiel's dry bones which symbolized God's people Israel (Ezekiel 37), and that it was present in Jesus and his disciples.

Unitarians would go further than this, and suggest that God's Spirit can inspire men and women in a multiplicity of ways, and not just in one single event. God's Spirit can move through the power of men and women's individual consciences; it can be seen in nature; it can be apprehended in the teachings of sages and prophets and indeed even through the thoughts and actions of seemingly ordinary people. The Spirit's inspiration can be found not only in the Judaeo-Christian tradition, but in any tradition where there is a sincere search for the truth. The Spirit can inspire both the loftier religious utterances of the prophet as well as those who would regard themselves as secular rather than religious: the 'green' campaigner or the CND leader can be just as spirit possessed (although they may not care to use such terminology), as someone who 'speaks in tongues' at a Pentecostalist service.

FESTIVALS OF OTHER FAITHS

The fact that Unitarians regard all traditions as potential sources of inspiration means that they are not confined to observing Judaeo-Christian festivals. It is quite common for Unitarians to recognize the fact that Christmas falls very close to the Jewish festival of Hanukah, the Festival of Lights, which commemorates the victory of the Maccabees over Antiochus in 175 BCE. One popular Unitarian hymn ('Our festival is here again') points to the juxtaposition of the Christian and Jewish festivals, and the common theme of light shining through darkness – a theme appropriate to the dark days of winter that everyone is experiencing at that time.

Festivals of other faiths are not systematically observed within the Unitarian movement. It is possible for a preacher to select the Sunday closest to Wesak (the festival of the

Buddha's birth, enlightenment and demise) as an occasion for reflecting on what the congregation might learn from Buddhist teachings. However, it is possible on any Sunday to draw on the spectrum of the world's religious traditions for readings, sermon themes and inspiration.

Inevitably different Unitarians will have different preferences about the traditions they find particularly inspiring, but it may be true to say that of the wide variety of religions which the world has to offer there are three at present that attract especial interest. Unitarians have particular affection for the religion of the Jews, being the cradle from which early Christianity was born and which, in common with Unitarianism, affirms the strict unity of God. Buddhism has also attracted much interest, perhaps because it has been perceived as the 'religion of reason' by virtue of its adamant rejection of accepting teachings through blind faith. More recently, Native American religion has come to the fore as a means of affirming earth-centred spirituality and the contribution which oppressed minority cultures have made to spiritual awareness and understanding.

Few Unitarians would go so far as to claim that all religions are equally edifying, or that they all teach the same truth. What they would believe is that there is no single religion which can claim the monopoly of religious truth or the sole and exclusive means of salvation. Each has something to offer: as George Matheson's hymn, enormously popular in Unitarian circles, puts it:

Each sees one colour in thy rainbow light,
Each looks upon one tint and calls it heaven;
Thou art the fullness of our partial sight;
We are not perfect till we find the seven.[3]

6 · UNITARIANS AND INTER-RELIGIOUS DIALOGUE

We have seen how Unitarians moved away from a belief in the authority of the Judaeo-Christian scriptures. However, if reason is the final authority in matters of doctrine, reason is a characteristic endowment of human beings everywhere not merely in the Judaeo-Christian tradition, or in Unitarian circles. Surely other faiths, then, have important elements of truth, and important insights on which one may draw.

James Martineau did not take his conclusions about 'the seat of authority' into the realm of other faiths; indeed he somewhat disapproved of the work of his pupil, J Estlin Carpenter (1844–1927), who was largely responsible for the modern British Unitarian interest in other religions. Whatever Martineau's reservations, Unitarians have had a long history of involvement with faiths outside the Judaeo-Christian tradition, and in this chapter I shall explore a number of key developments in this field.

THE MOROCCAN AMBASSADOR

The second written record in which the term 'Unitarian' is used (Chapter 1 mentioned the first) is a letter written in 1682 to the Moroccan ambassador in London, Ahmet Ben Abdullah. The two anonymous authors of the letter described themselves as 'belonging to that sect of Christians that are called Unitarians', and emphasized the points in common between their own belief in the oneness of God and the unitarianism of Islam and the Qur'an. The authors purport to speak on behalf of a wider sect bearing the Unitarian label, although, as we have seen, no church was actually designated 'Unitarian' until 1774.

The ambassador refused to accept the letter, realizing that its subject matter was religious in character. Nevertheless, the concept of the oneness of God has typically enabled Unitarians to find important points of contact with Jews and Muslims and opened doors considerably in advance of the more recent inter-faith dialogue movements within mainstream Christianity.

RAMMOHUN ROY (1772–1833)

The next substantial link with other faiths came almost a century and a half later with Rammohun Roy, who is sometimes said to have been the first serious student of world religions. Born in Radhanagar in Bengal, Roy studied Sanskrit, Bengali and Mathematics under a Hindu teacher, and Arabic and Persian from a Muslim. Persian was needed for service to the Moghul Emperor, but Roy also managed to learn some of the works of the Sufi poets. As Roy became acquainted with Islam, he became firmly drawn to the belief that there was only one God and that elaborate rituals, particularly those which involved the use of images, were wrong.

Having mastered Sanskrit, Roy was persuaded to go on to study at the University of Benares to further his studies of the Hindu scriptures. As he read Hindu philosophy, however, he came to the view that Hindu scriptures also taught a thorough-going monotheism. Roy found particular affinity with the Upanishads which affirmed that God was the absolute *brahman* (supreme soul) to be utterly contrasted with the plurality of forms and – particularly – images by means of which he was worshipped at a popular level. Roy also studied the Tantras, the Kalpa Sutras and some of the Jain scriptures.

Rammohun Roy wanted to recover the purity of the Hindu faith, as he believed it to be taught in the ancient Vedic scriptures. The worship of a pantheon of deities, the use of physical images, and all outward ritual and ceremonies, he believed, were totally superfluous. In 1815 he founded the *Atmuja Sabha*, the 'Society of the Spirit', where Hindus and Christians could worship together. The Unitarian congregation at Lewin's Mead in Bristol came to know of Roy's work, and made a financial donation to it.

One writer expresses surprise that:

> ... without seeing one Unitarian book, or conversing with any person of Unitarian views, he became a Unitarian Christian from the study of the Bible alone.[1]

Of course Roy was not a 'Unitarian Christian', and his unitarianism came from his Muslim-inspired monotheism. It should therefore come as no surprise that he arrived at his conviction about the unity of God without assistance from English Unitarians. Roy spoke of 'the Unitarianism of the Upanishads'; where the Upanishads appeared to suggest that there were several gods, he contended that this was allegorical.

Roy translated the Upanishads and other Vedic writings, and an abridged version was published in England, where they gained considerable acclaim. Indeed, when the celebrated scholar Max Müller read them he was inspired to study Sanskrit in order to understand them in the original. Rammohun Roy, he stated, was one of the greatest thinkers and religious reformers.

Meanwhile, in Calcutta, the Baptist Church had established its presence with a mission. William Carey and two colleagues had arrived from England and were struggling to learn Bengali and Sanskrit as a prelude to Bible translation work. They became close friends of Roy, who was glad to assist them.

The missionaries no doubt expected Roy to convert to Christianity, especially when he engaged in writing his now famous work *The Precepts of Jesus – The Guide to Peace and Happiness*. *The Precepts of Jesus* was simply a collection of passages from the four gospels, comprising sayings and teachings of Jesus. It is perhaps therefore surprising that this work should have aroused such controversy. The Christian missionaries were outraged by the book; indeed one Christian publicly accused him of arrogance 'to teach doctrines directly opposed to those held by the mass of real Christians in every age'.[2]

The problem about *The Precepts of Jesus* lay in what it omitted rather than what it stated. Roy could not accept the miracles of the New Testament, believing them to run contrary to reason which, he averred, was the supreme authority in determining religious truth. Religion, he held, was not to be equated with prejudice or superstition. Rational religion entailed the belief in one God and the acceptance of a moral code which would secure the orderly government of society. Roy was therefore happy to endorse Jesus' belief in a single deity and his moral discourses, but no more. Furthermore, Roy's firm belief in the unity of God caused him to find difficulties with the doctrine of the Trinity, much to the missionaries' disappointment. When they realized he was not going to convert, the missionaries regarded him as a 'heathen', and referred to him as such.

The Rev William Adam of the Baptist Mission, by contrast, was persuaded by Roy. He left the mission and sought Roy's help in forming the Calcutta Unitarian Committee. (Adam's apostasy earned him the nickname 'the second fallen Adam'!) This body was short lived, although it had the merit of attracting the interest of Unitarians in Britain and the United States.

Alas, the *Atmuja Sabha* proved too radical an endeavour for its time, and it dwindled in support. In 1828 Rammohun Roy established a new organization, the *Brahmo Samaj*, the members of which were known as the 'brotherhood', since they were admitted without respect for caste, status or nationality. The *Samaj* was a meeting ground for Indians and Europeans, for Hindus, Christians and Muslims. In 1833, Roy came to Bristol to visit Dr Lant Carpenter, minister of Lewin's Mead Unitarian Church, Bristol. Very soon after his arrival he became feverish, and was diagnosed as having meningitis. He died on 27 September 1833.

Although Rammohun Roy's visit to Bristol was short, Lant Carpenter's daughter, Mary (1807–77), was sufficiently impressed with Roy to go out to India herself. She was 60 years old when she first arrived, and made four visits in all. In Bristol she had done considerable work in children's education, and in India she founded a school for Hindu girls, and pressed for social reforms.

After Roy's death, one of his disciples, Keshab Chandar Sen (1838–84), took over the *Samaj* leadership. Like Roy, Sen affirmed the doctrine of God as revealed in conscience, and the manifestation of religion in moral behaviour. Sen leaned more towards Christianity than Roy, however, and introduced Christian practices such as prayer for the forgiveness of sins; he also permitted some elements of Hindu ceremonial. Sen advocated the ascetic life as an expression of religious devotion.

During Sen's period of office, there was a split in the *Samaj*. The traditionalists seceded to form the *Adi Brahmo Samaj*, which upheld more conservative Hindu practices, leaving Sen and his followers to press for inter-caste marriage, widow marriage and the abolition of caste. A number of prominent Hindus were constrained to join the *Brahmo Samaj* of India, as it came to be called, not least of which was Rabindranath Tagore (1861–1941).

J ESTLIN CARPENTER (1844–1927)

Joseph Estlin Carpenter was the grandson of Dr Lant Carpenter. He was named after Dr Estlin, who was the family physician who attended Rammohun Roy in his last days. Estlin decided to follow the family tradition of entering the

Unitarian ministry. He became minister of Oakfield Road Church in Clifton, Bristol, in 1886, and three years later of Mill Hill Chapel in Leeds, the former church of Joseph Priestley. In his ministerial years Estlin Carpenter had no particular claim to scholarship. He was a popularizer, although one of his congregation paid him the somewhat back-handed compliment of saying that a single morning service of Carpenter's was 'sufficient for a month'!

During his ministry at Mill Hill, Carpenter developed a serious speech impediment. There is some evidence that this may have been psychosomatic but, whatever its cause, it severely handicapped his work. His congregation sent him on an extended holiday and he travelled to Switzerland, Egypt and Palestine. When he returned, the situation was no better, despite the appointment of an assistant minister. In 1875 Carpenter resigned to take up an academic post: he was invited to become Professor of Ecclesiastical History, Comparative Religion and Hebrew at Manchester College, London. (Apparently a stammer was deemed to be acceptable to students, but not to a congregation!)

Notwithstanding Carpenter's credentials, he set to work to further his knowledge of Hebrew and Semitic studies, and began to learn Pali under the instruction of the eminent Buddhist scholar Dr T W Rhys Davids. Carpenter soon gained a national – indeed international – reputation in the field of biblical criticism and also in 'comparative religion', as the subject was then called.

Carpenter produced a remarkable literary output in this field. Among his achievements are *The Oxford Hexateuch*: a study of the first six books of the Old Testament in which he supports the Graf-Wellhausen hypothesis concerning the multiple authorship of these books. This work is summarized in Carpenter's contribution to the old (1919) edition of *Peake's Commentary on the Bible*. In the field of the New Testament, Carpenter wrote an important work entitled *The Johannine Writings*. His contributions to comparative religion included collaboration with Rhys Davids on his translation of the *Pali Canon* for the Pali Text Society: in fact, Carpenter was given sole responsibility for preparing the text of the third volume of the *Digha Nikaya*, an important Theravada Buddhist scripture.

Two particular original works of Carpenter are worth mentioning in the field of comparative religion. First, his *Comparative Religion* was pioneering in its quest for objectivity in a field which was cornered by Christian scholars keen to assert the superiority of Christianity over the 'non-Christian' faiths of the world. Carpenter openly criticized Sir Monier Williams for speaking of the 'three great false religions, Buddhism, brahmanism and Mohammedanism'.[3]

The other work of Carpenter is his collection of lectures entitled *Theism in Modern India*. These lectures were commissioned by the Hibbert Trust in 1919 (after Carpenter had retired from Manchester College), and delivered in the Essex Hall, off the Strand (the headquarters of the Unitarian Church). They are not only important in their own right as pioneering pieces of scholarship; they also attracted large numbers of laypeople, thus ensuring that the results of scholarship percolated down to a wider audience.

THE WORLD'S PARLIAMENT OF RELIGIONS

One major event, which effectively marked the birth of the inter-faith movement, was the World's Parliament of Religions. Held in Chicago in 1893, it attracted some 7,000 attendees from the world's major religions. Improved travel and communication, colonization and missionary enterprise had caused English to become the universal language. Chicago was chosen as the venue because it was the site of the World Exposition to mark the 400th anniversary of Columbus' 'discovery' of America. (The event was originally planned for 1892, but postponed for a year.) Exhibits were to be displayed which reflected the technological, commercial and cultural achievements of humanity. Charles Caroll Bonney, a Chicago lawyer and a Swedenborgian, however, argued that humanity's pinnacle of achievement was not technology, and that it would be appropriate to hold a large scale 'Parliament of Religions' concurrently with the Exposition.

Not only were the Unitarians present at the Parliament, but they also had a key role in its organization. The Secretary of the Parliament was a Unitarian minister by the name of Jenkin Lloyd Jones (1843–1918). Jones entered classes on world religions as part of his ministerial training in the late 1860s before becoming minister at Janesville, Wisconsin. In this first charge he became conscious that the Sunday School was very Bible-based, and he wished to challenge this policy. Accordingly Jones developed courses which embraced the sciences on the one hand and the founders of world religions on the other.

Jones moved to Chicago in 1884, to the Fourth Unitarian Church, renamed All Souls Church. Jones endeavoured to ensure that all souls were indeed welcome to his congregation. In one of his sermons he declared:

> Into our fellowship no one will ever be prevented to come by doctrinal bar; here at least let no man be a stranger, who chooses to stand within our gates, let him be Jew, Gentile or Agnostic, Mohammedan or Buddhist, Infidel or Atheist so long as he desires to share with us the burden bearing, the life helping, the love extending duties he is welcome.[4]

Jones became editor of *Unity*, the mouthpiece of the Unitarian denomination, and introduced the practice of publishing articles on world religions. The editorial office of *Unity*, as it happened, was in the same building as Bonney's law office.

There was a third key figure associated with the Parliament: the Rev J H Barrows, Pastor of the First Presbyterian Church of Chicago. Having been elected Secretary to the Parliament, Jones was much surprised that Barrows took control by taking the Chair. No doubt this was a strategic move to forestall hostility amongst Christians. The then Archbishop of Canterbury, for example, had expressed his lack of support for the Parliament on the grounds that it granted an equality of status to each participating religion, which he could not accept. Although tolerant of other religions, Barrows viewed Christianity as the culmination of all other faiths, and believed that inter-religious encounter would enable 'the best religion [to] come to the front'.⁵ (Bonney was prepared to give them 'parity of esteem'.)

Many religious celebrities came from all over the globe. Amongst the famous names were Anagarika Dharmapala (responsible for the revival of Sinhalese Buddhism as a backlash to Christian missionary activity) and Swami Vivekenanda. Max Müller and J Estlin Carpenter were invited, but neither was able to attend: they both sent papers, which were read to the assembled gathering.

Although the Parliament stipulated that participants should not openly criticize other faiths, this did not result in bland platitudes on the part of the speakers. On the contrary, a number of speakers stated boldly what they regarded as the merits of their own faith, and particularly the Christian evangelicals vociferously argued the case for Christian triumphalism. Indeed, a distinctively English-speaking and Christian ethos pervaded the Parliament: it opened with Psalm 100, complete with Trinitarian doxology, followed by the Lord's Prayer, and the gathering concluded with 'Lift up your heads, O ye gates'.

However, despite the high profile accorded to Christianity, the World's Parliament of Religions enabled Eastern faiths to be presented as serious alternatives in a population to whom they had hitherto been virtually unknown. Minds were opening to new horizons, and indeed one of the Japanese attendees, Soen Shaku, so inspired an influential publisher called Paul Carus, that Carus invited D T Suzuki, Soen Shaku's pupil, to come and work for his publishing house.⁶ Suzuki went on to publish prolifically on Zen Buddhism, and has been avidly read by Westerners over the past few decades.

THE IARF

One permanent outcome of the World's Parliament of Religions was the formation of the International Association for Religious Freedom. It was founded in 1900, and its first secretary was Dr Charles William Wendte (1844–1931).

Wendte's parents converted to Unitarianism when they came to the USA on their honeymoon. One Sunday they went to a church which was unknown to them and were impressed by the service. 'That was real common sense,' Mr Wendte is reported to have said. 'Fancy hearing something sensible from a preacher!' It was a Unitarian church: when their first son was born, Mr Wendte stated, 'We want him to become a Unitarian minister'.[7]

The organization was originally called the International Council of Unitarian and other Liberal Religious Thinkers and Workers. After various name changes, the title 'International Association for Religious Freedom' (IARF) was chosen for the Congress in Boston in 1969 – the name which the organization has retained ever since. The new name opened the door to religions other than Christianity: member groups include the Japanese Buddhist group the Rissho Kosei-kai, the Brahmo Samaj of Bangladesh and India, the Guru Nanak Foundation, and the Ramakrishna Institute. In more recent times, traditional primal religions have come to be represented, as well as humanists.[8] At present, roughly half of its members are Unitarians. The IARF is affiliated to the United Nations, Unesco and Unicef, and organizes emergency relief work through its Social Service Network.

JAMES FREEMAN CLARKE (1810–88)
R TRAVERS HERFORD (1860–1950)

Two other Unitarian scholars deserve brief mention. We have already mentioned James Freeman Clarke in the context of American Unitarianism. Clarke is better known, however, for his famous two-volume work *Ten Great Religions: an Essay in Comparative Theology* (1871). Although most of his working life was spent in congregational ministry, with some time as General Secretary of the AUA, Clarke was a professor at Harvard from 1867 to 1871. Surprising as it may seem, 'comparative religion' was something of a sideline for Clarke, who wrote much more prolifically on wider theological issues. He published 32 books, and over 1,000 articles and sermons.

Clarke's Transcendentalist leanings enabled him to look beyond Christianity to the religions of the East, and *Ten Great Religions* spans all the major religions of the world, apart from Jainism and Sikhism. These religions are compared with Christianity on a number of themes: God, the soul, life after death, prayer, worship and salvation. Despite his catholicity, Clarke still believed that Christianity was supreme: he criticized Hinduism for its belief in caste, Buddhism for its absence of God, and Islam for its predestinarianism. He saw these and other religions as stages on a journey, in preparation for a new absolute religion, based on the Christian faith, which would transcend them.

It is Clarke who was responsible for a five-point summary of Unitarianism, which one still occasionally finds displayed in Unitarian churches. He called it 'Five Points of the New Theology':

The Fatherhood of God
The Brotherhood of Man
The Leadership of Jesus
Salvation by Character
The Continuity of Human Development ... or the Progress
    of Mankind, onward and upward for ever.

R Travers Herford was another Unitarian minister, who furthered inter-faith relations in Britain. He is less well known than Clarke, but his work on the Jewish faith is nonetheless impressive. Herford started to learn Hebrew when he was 13 years old, and became interested not merely in the Hebrew scriptures, but in first-century Judaism and the Talmud. His writings include *Pharisaism* (1921) and *The Idea of the Kingdom of God* (1924), works which much impressed the Reform Jewish scholar Leo Baeck.

Herford has been unduly neglected. His belief that knowledge of first-century Judaism can shed important light on early Christianity was much ahead of its time, and has only in the last ten years or so gained prominence amongst Jewish and Christian scholars. Herford's work was not exclusively academic: he described himself as a 'Jewnitarian', and did much to champion Jewish rights against anti-semitism.

HAVE UNITARIANS A CHRISTIAN IDENTITY?

All this implies that Unitarians have long since moved beyond the dilemma about whether to follow reason or to follow (Judaeo-Christian) scripture. A much more real dilemma today is whether Unitarians should identify themselves with their historical Christian origins, or whether the three-fold principle of freedom, reason and tolerance implies that they have moved beyond it to a more ecumenical and perhaps eclectic position. As one might expect, there are different views on this question. Some Unitarians, particularly in the USA, would say categorically that they are not Christian; indeed, one writer estimates that only 20 per cent of American Unitarians regard themselves as Christian.[9] By contrast, Hungarian and Transylvanian Unitarians would be much more likely to claim a Christian identity: their form of Unitarianism is much more traditional, with a Bible-based liturgy. The same is true of the Non-subscribing Presbyterian Church of Ireland. British Unitarians come somewhere between these two extremes; although no firm statistics are available, roughly half of British Unitarians would see themselves as Christian, while the other half would not.

As one might also expect, there are different reasons for claiming or rejecting a Christian identity. Some Unitarians believe that the emphasis on the Christian tradition, as compared with that of other world religions, is insufficiently great to allow them to be counted as Christian any longer. For others, the problem is more of an etymological one: the name 'Christian' implies 'follower of Christ', and the word 'Christ' presents a problem. These Unitarians feel that they can believe in the human Jesus as a teacher and an example to follow, but to accord him the title of 'Christ' implies either some supernatural status (the one who is risen and has ascended into heaven from whence he rules the world) or some special unique chosenness by God, like the personal messiah whom certain Jews have expected.

So is Unitarianism Christian or not? One Unitarian recently suggested that an appropriate description would be 'post-Christian'. Unitarianism's past has been formed and shaped by Christianity, but Unitarians today have moved beyond it into something much wider. As he put it, 'Some of our members and friends may well regard themselves as Christians in a broad sense, but that is no longer the predominant stance among us. If anything, I suppose, our position could be described as post-Christian, since while most of us acknowledge our Christian roots we feel we have moved beyond them'.[10]

Whether Unitarians are Christians, then, depends on how one looks at it. If one understands 'Christian' to mean someone who accepts Jesus Christ as the unique and final revelation of God, the second member of the Trinity, the saviour of the world who offered his life on the cross as an atoning sacrifice for sin, who miraculously rose again from the dead and ascended into heaven, where he sits at God's right hand, and will judge the living and the dead, then the answer is clear: most Unitarians cannot subscribe to such doctrines, and none is expected to do so.

However, there are other ways in which one's claim to a Christian identity might be measured. One such yardstick might be one's degree of acceptance by mainstream Christian denominations. In Britain, the situation is somewhat uncertain. In 1992, the British Council of Churches (BCC) reorganized itself as a result of the Roman Catholics' willingness to become part of an ecumenical body. The BCC became the Council of Churches for Britain and Ireland (CCBI). Previously the Unitarians had belonged to the BCC as 'Associate Members': that is to say, representatives might attend meetings and participate in BCC events, but had no voting rights. When the BCC became the CCBI, Unitarians applied for full membership. They were not accepted, although they were recommended to apply for 'observer status'. Again they were turned down, although the Society of Friends (the Quakers) were accepted. The Quakers were disappointed with this decision, since Quakers and Unitarians have regarded themselves as having much in common. However, Unitarians will continue to work with mainstream Christians wherever this is possible, with or without formal acceptance.

In the USA the situation is much clearer. They do not belong to mainstream Church councils, and at the 1997 General Assembly, UUs pledged themselves to co-operate actively with other faiths.

7 · SOCIAL CONCERNS

The Unitarian emphasis on reason as a fundamental principle often gives rise to the supposition that Unitarians are cold rationalists, over-intellectual and incapable of feeling. One suspects that those who perceive Unitarianism as a kind of religious debating society simply do not know the denomination at all well. On the contrary, Unitarians have been heavily involved in social and political matters, perhaps even more so than theological ones. 'Deeds not creeds' was a recent slogan found on many Unitarian notice boards in Britain. More surprising, perhaps, is the fact that, although Unitarianism encourages much diversity in its members' outlook, Unitarians have enjoyed a extraordinary measure of agreement on social issues.

Unitarians have been remarkably prominent in public life. No less than five US Presidents have been Unitarians: John Adams (1735–1826), Thomas Jefferson (1743–1826), John Quincy Adams (1767–1848), Millard Fillmore (1800–74) and William Howard Taft (1857–1930). Jefferson, of course, was responsible for writing the famous American Declaration of Independence. In Unitarian circles, he is also known for his *Jefferson Bible*, which is a harmonization of the four gospels, skilfully combined in such a way as to remove not only the repetitions, but all miraculous elements. Jefferson's text simply ends with an account of Jesus' burial, without any reference to the resurrection. His aim was to present the 'philosophy of Jesus' in a reasonable way.

Other famous Unitarians have included the geologist Sir Charles Lyell (1797–1875), and George Stephenson (1781–1848), the builder of the first steam locomotive. Samuel Morse (1791–1872), the inventor of the electric telegraph and the famous Morse Code, was a Unitarian, as were Alexander Graham Bell (1847–1922), who invented the telephone, and Tim Berners-Lee (*b*1955), inventor of the World Wide Web – three of the most prominent figures in modern communication.

Unitarianism has had more than its fair share of writers, who have included: novelists Elizabeth Gaskell (1810–65), Charles Dickens (1812–70), Herman Melville (1819–91), and Louisa May Alcott (1832–88); essayists William Hazlitt (1778–1830) and Charles Lamb (1775–1834); poets e e cummings (1894–1962), Robert Burns (1759–96), and Henry W Longfellow (1807–82); and children's writer Beatrix Potter (1866–1943). In the world of music, Béla Bartók (1881–1945) and Sir Adrian Boult (1899–1983) were both Unitarians. Albert Schweitzer (1875–1965), who in a single life span combined New Testament scholarship, medicine and expertise at the organ, once stated that he regarded himself as a Unitarian.

Sometimes Unitarians are accused of wishing to appropriate 'famous names', claiming that they are Unitarians, even when their links with the movement are tenuous. There was a short period in which Unitarians wanted to claim Gene Roddenberry (1921–91), the author of *Star Trek,* as one of their own. When Roddenberry died, a UU minister – Ray Bradbury – gave the eulogy at his funeral, and some saw Unitarian ideas in the television series (its optimism, opportunities for women, and so on). However, Roddenberry never joined a Unitarian church, and once accepted an award as 'Humanist of the Year', so the British Humanist Association, which claims Roddenberry as a humanist, probably has a better case than the Unitarians!

Unitarians may have been prone to exaggerate the membership of their Hall of Fame, but equally there are historical figures who have been Unitarians, but who concealed their religious identity for fear of disapproval, sometimes preferring the more general designation 'Christian'. In many cases, standard reference works simply fail to mention religious affiliations in their entries. The 'Unitarians' mentioned in this chapter are therefore Unitarians in different senses of the word. Yet, whatever the nature of their links, it is undoubtedly true that Unitarians have produced an undue preponderance of men and women who have made important contributions to society. Indeed, the well-known writer Vance Packard said, 'The Unitarian Church, tiny in total number, outranks all denominations in the number of eminent Americans who have claimed it as their Church'.[1]

There are no doubt various reasons why this is the case. The Unitarian emphasis on reason has, first of all, ensured that those who find their way into the denomination have a fairly high standard of intelligence and a good education, qualities which may have given them the edge in their achievements in the arts and the sciences. The emphasis on reason, as we have seen, has also entailed a belief in the essential worth of the individual, and this has given momentum for their work for social causes. Particularly with regard to social conditions, Unitarians have sought to ensure that their convictions would reach as wide an audience as possible: hence the attempts of Charles Dickens and Mrs Gaskell to expose the plight of the poor and their exploitation by the rich. Readers of Dickens are seldom aware of his Unitarian leanings, but a story such as *A Christmas Carol*, to take but one example, illustrates the Unitarian notion of original virtue: even Scrooge, who seems unredeemable, can mend his ways and finally emerge as a truly reformed person.

Finally, the absence of any repressive authority, such as the traditional Roman Catholic Church, ensured that Unitarians enjoyed free expression and permission to explore new ideas, wherever they might lead. This has no doubt served to encourage creativity and ensured that new ideas were not stifled.

HUMANITARIAN CAUSES

Unitarians were one of the first religious groups to bring politics into the religious arena. Before the 18th century it was not the done thing for clergy to preach 'political' sermons. When an event of national importance occurred, such as the outbreak of a war, the government would call a 'Fast Day', on which the clergy would be expected to preach in support of government policy, offering strength and encouragement to the congregation. Even the Unitarians tended to confine political comment almost exclusively to matters of religious liberty. (Unitarians championed the cause of religious freedom not only for themselves, but on behalf of Roman Catholics, Jews and agnostics.) However, there were a number of Unitarian preachers who used the pulpit for political as well as religious matters: early examples were Theophilus Lindsey, Thomas Belsham, Richard Price (1723–91) and Robert Aspland (1782–1845), among others.

POLITICS AND ELECTORAL REFORM

Unitarians have had little sympathy with the view, sometimes expressed by evangelical Christians, that a religious believer should definitely leave politics alone. Unitarians have been highly active in the political arena for several centuries, at local and at national level. In Britain, the cities of Leeds, Leicester and Birmingham have seen the beneficial effects of several Unitarian mayors and councillors, spanning education, public health, public services such as libraries, and better amenities such as purer water and cheaper gas.

In Britain the Unitarians contributed greatly to parliamentary reform in the last two centuries. The theory of 'natural rights', championed by the philosopher John Locke (1632–1732) – who is often regarded as a Unitarian – created awareness that life, liberty and property were basic entitlements of human beings, and not privileges afforded only to the more fortunate of society.

ECONOMICS AND INDUSTRY

Several famous inventors have been Unitarians. Examples include Jedediah Strutt (1726–97) who collaborated in the spinning frame's development. Josiah Wedgwood (1730–95) invented new, now world-famous, ways of making pottery, which were so innovative that his employees had to sign an oath of secrecy about his methods.

Unitarians were instrumental in founding the Manchester Statistical Society in 1833, which was followed by similar societies in London and Bristol, in 1834 and 1836 respectively. Although statistics may seem far removed from religion, it was only through statistical evidence that the full extent of Britain's social problems could be ascertained. It should be remembered that in 1801 – the date of the first British census – no one even knew the approximate size of Britain's population. Richard Price used statistics for the calculation of life insurance and old age pensions. He helped to found The Equitable Society in 1762, thus putting the insurance industry on a proper actuarial basis. Until then, insurance premiums had been arrived at largely by guesswork. Price's seminal work, *Observations on Reversionary Payments* (1769) is found alongside his more distinctively theological writings.

In later years, Charles Booth (1840–1916) – also a Unitarian – was able to use the new statistical science to undertake an important survey of Britain's social conditions, and Florence Nightingale (1820-1910), who was born into a Unitarian family, was able to impress the Home Office by providing them with statistical information to support her cause. (Florence Nightingale is usually renowned for her work in caring for soldiers in the Crimean War, but she was also the inventor of the pie chart!)

Unitarians were instrumental in campaigning against child labour in factories, where conditions were appalling. John Fielden (1784–1849), a Unitarian, worked in his father's factory from the age of ten onwards, and hence was a child labourer himself. Later in life he became the factory's owner and a Member of Parliament. Fielden's work *The Curse of the*

Factory System (1836) was highly influential in raising public consciousness about the plight of children in factories. He supported a Ten Hours' Bill (1847), which significantly limited the hours of child labour, despite the full knowledge that this would lose him his parliamentary seat.

PUBLIC HEALTH

Unitarians have achieved much in the field of public health, and in this regard Thomas Southwood Smith (1788–1861) is particularly worthy of mention. Smith obtained a scholarship to study for the ministry, but gave it up when his wife died, and turned to medicine as a career, graduating with an MD in 1816. During his period of medical studies Smith took charge of the Edinburgh Unitarian congregation, and succeeded in increasing weekly attendance there from 20 to an amazing 200! He played a prominent part in the formation of the Scottish Unitarian Association, which was founded in 1813.

After a short spell in Yeovil, Smith settled in London in 1820, where he continued his career in medicine, preaching only occasionally. He was particularly interested in epidemics which were still only too common, and wrote *A Treatise on Fever* in 1830. Previously it had been believed that diseases such as cholera and yellow fever were contagious, and that sufferers must be put into quarantine. Smith demonstrated, however, that insanitary conditions were the main factors leading to the spread of these diseases, and that they were therefore avoidable. He brought pressure on local government to ensure better housing conditions: he visited all the clergy in East London, as well as the Bishop of London, calling on them for support. Smith also knew Charles Dickens, who lent his support too.

In 1824, Smith published a work entitled *The Use of the Dead to the Living*, in which he defended his belief that the dissection of corpses was an important means of improving medical knowledge and ascertaining causes of death. At that time there was a great deal of prejudice against this, which Smith sought to overcome. The philosopher Jeremy Bentham (1748–1832), often regarded as a Unitarian, was one of Smith's supporters in this regard: not only had he declared in his will that he wished his body to be used for medical research, but he actually bequeathed his corpse to Smith, who dissected it publicly, accompanied by a lecture on anatomy. While the lecture was taking place, a loud thunderstorm broke out, which even Smith found disconcerting. His audience reported that he continued to lecture and dissect, but with a face almost as ashen as that of Bentham's corpse! Bentham's skeleton was preserved, and still remains in University College, London.

SLAVERY

One area of social concern which affected Unitarians was the issue of slavery. Although numerous Unitarians had a highly influential role in securing the abolition of the slave trade and slave ownership, their track record on this issue could certainly have been better. Concern about the institution of slavery is not one of Unitarianism's 'firsts': the original campaigners in the USA were in fact Mennonites and Quakers.

One might have thought that it ought to have been self-evident that slavery was a grave wrong, given Unitarian views about the inherent worth of human beings, and the American Constitution's statement, drafted by a Unitarian President, that 'all men are created equal'. By the 19th century, some 15 million black people had been brought against their will to the Western hemisphere but, sadly, many people's vested interests (including those of Unitarians) aroused strong opposition to the abolitionist cause, particularly in the cotton growing areas in the south of the USA. Of all the Unitarian clergy, it was the Transcendentalists who were the most vocal. This may seem surprising, in view of their 'nature mysticism', but their emphasis on conscience enabled them to place social justice higher than either the law of the land or material vested interests.

The Transcendentalists were not the only supporters of abolitionism. In 1830 William Lloyd Garrison (1805–79), a Unitarian, founded the Anti-Slavery Society. William Ellery

William Ellery Channing wrote a book entitled *Slavery* (1835), in which he spoke of it as 'barbarism'. Ezra Stiles Gannett (1801–71) described it as 'the greatest evil under which our nation labours'.[2] Channing advocated sending American blacks back to Africa, and Channing advocated that the government should compensate slave owners and secure education for freed slaves. Channing was opposed by his own congregation.

Of all Unitarians, it is Theodore Parker who deserves particular mention for his work in this area. Parker believed that it was not sufficient simply to recognize the moral precepts of Jesus and proclaim them from the pulpit. Jesus' moral teachings had to be put into practice. Accordingly, from his base in his new church in Boston, Parker engaged in much work on temperance, prison reform, the education of women, and – most especially – the Boston Anti-Slavery Crusade. He wrote anti-slavery tracts such as *A Letter to the People of the United States Touching the Matter of Slavery* (1848). He actively helped fugitive slaves to escape, and he served on the secret committee which assisted the famous John Brown, the famous abolitionist martyr – whose 'soul goes marching on'! – who armed a number of slaves by raiding the Federal armoury at Harpers Ferry in 1859.

In 1843 the AUU General Assembly passed a resolution against slavery. However, slaves were not finally emancipated until the end of the American Civil War. Finally, in 1865, the Thirteenth Amendment to the American Constitution was passed, which ended the institution of slavery.

Meanwhile, back in England many entrepreneurs – including a number of Unitarians – owned slaves abroad. Robert Hibbert (founder of the Hibbert Trust) is said to have owned 400 slaves in Jamaica. Black servants, although technically not 'slaves', experienced conditions that were little better. In 1788 the Rev John Yates, a Unitarian minister in Liverpool, caused deep offence to many of his congregation by preaching against it. In the same year, Joseph Priestley preached a sermon with a similar message. His congregation was more favourably disposed towards it, and requested that it should be published. Apparently copies sold well.

Unitarian abolitionist campaigners in 19th-century Britain included Unitarian MP William Roscoe (1753–1831), Josiah Wedgwood, Jeremy Bentham and Lant Carpenter. Roscoe's vote in Parliament against the institution cost him his seat. The year 1823 heralded the Anti-Slavery Society, chaired by William Smith, a Unitarian. Ten years later a law was introduced to free all slaves. Owners were obliged to ensure a period of apprenticeship for them, and entrepreneurs were to be entitled to compensation.

EDUCATION

Of all the work done by Unitarians in society, education is perhaps the area that stands out most. There are several reasons why Unitarians have typically shown a commitment to education: the high regard paid to human reason is one, and education is the means by which one can raise public consciousness of other social matters, and of the causes of social ills. One argument against universal suffrage was that the populace at large was too ignorant to be allowed to select its political leaders; hence the Unitarians' answer to the problem was to ensure better public education. Education thus might be said to underpin the Unitarians' programme of social reform.

Unitarians have contributed to all levels of education – university, adult education, day schools, night schools, Sunday schools and women's schools – and they helped to establish public libraries.[3] The famous Tate Gallery in London, and the Tate Library in Harris Manchester College, Oxford, are named after Sir Henry Tate (1819–99), a Unitarian.

Being unable to subscribe to the Church of England's Thirty-Nine Articles, Unitarians were ineligible for education at Oxford and Cambridge Universities. Non-conformists who wished to undertake higher education therefore had to devise their own alternatives. One of the first of these was Warrington Academy, at which Joseph Priestley was at one time a tutor. Warrington Academy became Manchester Academy (1786), and finally moved to Oxford to become

Manchester College, Oxford (now Harris Manchester College). Until recently, Manchester College's main purpose was the training of ministerial candidates for the Unitarian Church; although this function still continues in a very small degree, Harris Manchester College now caters principally for mature students, allowing adult returners the possibility of obtaining a University of Oxford degree. Other universities in whose founding Unitarians have been instrumental include Manchester, Liverpool, Birmingham, Sheffield and Leeds, and the University Colleges of Leicester and Nottingham.

The Unitarians were not exclusively interested in the educational 'high flyers'. As we have seen, their concern for poverty encompassed a concern for the education of the poor. To achieve this, the Unitarians pioneered the 'ragged schools', the first of which was founded in 1818 by John Pounds (1766–1839). As a youth, Pounds was apprenticed as a shipwright in Portsmouth, England; after falling into a dry dock he was left severely crippled, and turned to shoemaking instead. In 1818 he was given the responsibility of looking after his five-year-old nephew while his brother was at sea. Pounds discovered that he related well to children and was a good teacher. Other children were added to his charge, and within a short time he was tutoring a total of 40, including 12 girls. This was Pounds' first 'ragged school'; unable to employ staff, he taught all the pupils himself. His curriculum consisted of reading, arithmetic, cooking, handicrafts and, understandably, shoe-mending! Dr Thomas Guthrie in his *Plea for Ragged Schools* (1847) named Pounds as their originator.

DOMESTIC MISSIONS

One important Unitarian innovation was the 'domestic mission', an idea that stemmed from Dr Joseph Tuckerman (1778–1840) of Boston, USA. Contrary to the common belief that churches were full in 19th-century Britain, the 1851 Religious Census revealed that only about half the British population attended church with any regularity. In particular, the poorer members of the population, for various reasons, were alienated from the churches and were the least likely to attend. Knowing that a large sector of the population did not come to church to hear the Christian message, Unitarians determined that they should take their message from the church to people's homes, particularly those of the poor. In 1831 the first domestic missionary was appointed, and in 1835 the first domestic mission building was erected.

The Unitarians' message was not confined to religion. James Kitson (1807–1885), for example, gave lessons on hygiene to some of the working women of Leeds, and the missions typically gave advice on means of self-improvement, savings schemes, clothing clubs and reading rooms.

POSITION OF WOMEN

One of the most important Unitarian contributions to societal issues is their attitude to women. As early as 1792, Mary Wollstonecraft (1759–97), a Unitarian, wrote her *Vindication of the Rights of Women*. It was only to be expected that Unitarians, with few exceptions, would find themselves in support of women's rights. Even before the suffrage movement gathered momentum from the 1850s onwards, the South Place Chapel in Finsbury, London, had become a nucleus for female emancipation. The Rev William Johnson Fox (1786–1864) had gained himself a reputation for what were at the time extreme views on women's suffrage, and on women's positions regarding marriage and divorce. (Fox also had the distinction of preaching the sermon at Bentham's funeral.)

Alas, Fox was somewhat too far ahead of his time, even for other Unitarians: he alienated himself from other Unitarian clergy and from many of his congregation, and the South Place Chapel was formally excluded from the denomination. However, on both sides of the Atlantic, Unitarians of both genders involved themselves in the women's suffrage movement. Names like Susan Brownell Anthony (1820–1906), Mary Livermore (1820–1905) and Lucy Stone (1818–93) stand out as American campaigners, and Dr Emily Stowe (1831–1903), a women's rights leader, achieved the distinction of becoming the first woman school principal in Canada, and subsequently practised as a doctor.

Mention must be made of the ordination of women. The Unitarians and the Universalists were the first two denominations to remove any bar to women entering the ministry. The Unitarians recognized that, if reason was a universal endowment of human beings, then it was equally present in women and men, and that 'the priesthood of all believers' should encompass both genders. The ministry of women in worship first gained its rise in the American Universalist tradition, when Maria Cook (1779–1835) preached at Bainbridge, New York, in 1811. Cook received a number of preaching engagements, but her sermons appear to have focused on defending her right to preach. According to accounts, her sermons became increasingly dull, with the inevitable result that invitations dwindled, and finally she gave up preaching altogether.

Olympia Brown (1835–1926) was the first woman to become formally ordained in the Universalist Church; indeed she is probably the first to have become ordained in the history of Judaeo-Christianity! This took place in 1863, 60 years before women were allowed to vote in the USA. She left the ministry at the age of 35 to support the cause of women's suffrage.

Gertrud von Petzold is generally cited as the first woman minister in Britain, having become ordained in 1904. This claim, however, has been questioned by Glasgow Unitarians, who point to the Rev Caroline Soule, who was ordained there in 1880, in the congregation's former Universalist days. At that time, links between the two denominations were close, and Soule preached at, and subsequently served as pastor of, the Dundee Unitarian Church.

Women's energies have extended beyond women's rights. Margaret Barr (1897–1973) is one example who must be mentioned for her work amongst the Indians of the Khasi Hills. The Khasi Indians were not Hindus: they had settled from Cambodia, where they had practised a form of primal shamanism. Christian missionaries converted them to Welsh Calvinism, but one tribesman, Hajjor Kissor Singh, had begun to question their doctrines. In 1887 a missionary from the Brahmo Samaj visited the Hills, and aroused Singh's interest. At the missionary's suggestion, Singh wrote to Jabez Sunderland, an American Unitarian missionary, who provided him with tracts and materials. The following year Singh was able to form a small 'Unitarian Union'.

The movement grew, and the Unitarians felt it was desirable to send out a teacher to offer support. After overcoming the difficulty of persuading the denomination to send out a woman, Margaret Barr, who was a trained teacher, spent some 35 years organizing schools for the children, as well as health care. Although remote, the Khasi Hills Unitarians continue to gain the support and affection of Unitarians world-wide.

'THE GREATEST SHOW ON EARTH'

One further celebrated personality in the UU tradition deserves brief mention. He is Phineas Taylor Barnum (1801–91), the famous founder of Barnum's Circus, billed as 'The Greatest Show on Earth'. In 1842 Barnum purchased a museum in New York City, where he was the first showman to introduce 'freak shows'. The famous 'General Tom Thumb', who was only 25 inches tall, was one of his exhibits. Influenced by some of the evolutionist ideas of his time, and especially the concept of 'the great chain of being', Barnum devised many kinds of 'missing links' for his exhibition, including his 'Fiji Mermaid', which appeared to be half monkey, half fish. Needless to say, most of the exhibits were fakes! Barnum also introduced beauty contests, which drew in the public. When he was over 60 years old, he branched out into the circus, his particular innovations being his flamboyant introductions to the acts, and his use of three rings instead of one.

If he were judged by today's standards, Barnum might well be the object of Unitarian protests rather than adulation. Circuses are no longer 'politically correct', of course, and today's UUs would be far more eager to help the disabled than to degrade them by making them into curiosities to be laughed at. Barnum at least demonstrates, however, the world-affirming nature of UUs: in contrast with those forms of religion which advocate austerity and separation from the world, UUs see no problem in enjoying life and having a good time. In fairness to Barnum, it should be said he also did provide more wholesome forms of entertainment, such as the theatre, and he had the distinction of being the first to open a display aquarium.

Barnum wrote a short booklet, *Why I am a Universalist* (1895), which indicates the sincerity of his convictions. He also worked assiduously for the temperance movement. One Sunday he heard a sermon on temperance and was persuaded by it. He came home and poured his collection of finest wines down the drain! Unitarians in Britain and the USA have lent their support to the temperance movement. Most have interpreted 'temperance' in its literal sense of moderation, and have advocated either that people should not drink to excess, or that they should avoid distilled spirits. A few Unitarians, like Barnum, however, took temperance to entail total abstinence.

THE FLAMING CHALICE

Today Unitarians continue to work for society in a variety of ways. In Britain the General Assembly has an Office of Social Responsibility which aims to promote social action in a variety of areas: social justice, racial justice, peace, the AIDS epidemic, to name but a few. Unitarians and UUs world-wide have similar concerns.

The Unitarian-UU symbol of the flaming chalice is a powerful reminder of Unitarian social involvements. It was devised during the Second World War, when the Rev Charles Joy, Director of the Unitarian Service Committee, was attempting to assist refugees – mainly Jews – to escape from the Nazis. The organization needed a symbol to ensure recognition on official documents, and a Czech refugee cartoonist, Hans Deutsch, was commissioned to design an appropriate logo. The 'flaming chalice' was the result.

Some Unitarians see the flaming chalice as a reminder of the early Czech Reformer John Huss (c1372–1415), who was burnt at the stake for extending the communion chalice to the laity. (The Roman Catholic Church, until Vatican II, allowed only the priests to receive the elements in 'both kinds'.) The flame thus serves as a reminder of Huss' martyrdom.

In many Unitarian churches, the Sunday service begins with the lighting of a chalice – a powerful reminder of Unitarian tradition and service.

8 · THE EDGES OF TOLERANCE

Erasmus Darwin, the grandfather of Charles Darwin, was a friend of Joseph Priestley, and a member of Priestley's Lunar Society. Darwin has been described as a 'deeply religious man'; at one point in his life he attended services at the Unitarian chapel at Shrewsbury, but never actually embraced Unitarianism, which he described as 'a feather-bed for falling Christians'.[1] It is understandable that, to some who are outside the movement, Unitarianism may seem to be a soft option for those who are unable to subscribe to the creeds and dogmas of mainstream Christianity, a religion where 'anything goes' and where all are accepted, whatever their beliefs or practices.

The line between tolerance and anarchy is a fine one. The spirit of freedom and the spirit of chaos are all too closely related, and it is therefore not surprising that many Unitarians would regard some forms of intellectual quest as going beyond the scope of the freedom, reason and tolerance which are the bywords of the Unitarians.

How tolerant should tolerance be? What are Unitarians to say of the New Age phenomenon which has gathered momentum since the 1980s? How are they to regard the spirituality of paganism, Wicca and 'goddess religion'? What about spiritualism and psychic phenomena? Are these spurious forms of intellectual enquiry, or are they worthy of at least some consideration?

The problem that many Unitarians find with such paths is that there may be occasions when the spirit of freedom and tolerance collides with the principle of reason. Not everything is reasonable and, as we have seen, Unitarianism took its rise against blind credulity and unsupported doctrines which had simply been taken for granted by mainstream Christianity. On the other hand, the principle of reason is only one of the movement's three chief principles, and many Unitarians would insist that the denomination is not the cold rationalist organization which many believe it is.

In this chapter, I shall consider a number of movements that have arisen within Unitarian circles, and comment on their place within the denomination. First, there are New Age, pagan and earth-centred Unitarians. Second, there are Unitarians who are interested in psychic and paranormal phenomena. Third, there exists a body within the movement of self-styled atheists and humanists.

ATTITUDES TO THE NEW AGE: RALPH WALDO EMERSON AND THE TRANSCENDENTALIST MOVEMENT

Attitudes to the 'New Age' and earth-centred spirituality are inevitably mixed amongst Unitarians. While some members may see New Age ideas as highlighting things we do not yet understand, others regard them as superstition and self-deception. Historically, nature-spirituality has found a place within the Unitarian movement, even in its earlier stages, and Unitarianism might have become equated with cold rationalism if it had not been for Ralph Waldo Emerson (1803–82). Emerson was a Unitarian minister at the Second Church in Boston. He resigned his charge after preaching a sermon about the sacrament of communion, in which he argued that it was an unnecessary aid to the spiritual life. Emerson's problems with organized religion were in fact much wider than this: he believed that the one true teacher was not a church, a sacred book, sacred rites or even an academic establishment like a university, but rather the world itself. Emerson left Boston for England, where he sought out the English Romantics, such as Coleridge, Carlyle and Wordsworth. He hoped that organized religion might become displaced by Romantic spirituality.

Emerson returned to the USA in 1834, and in the same year published his important essay entitled *Nature*. In this he argued that nature is the true teacher, not books, universities or churches. Emerson once had a dream, in which he saw a large globe, representing the world, initially large, but which gradually contracted until it had reduced itself to the size of an apple. A voice seemed to command Emerson to eat the apple, and he obeyed. Thus Emerson – at least figuratively speaking – ate the world! The import of the dream is that the world was one both with himself and with God. As Emerson taught, 'I am part or particle of God'.[2]

The idea that the soul is ultimately one with God has its affinities, of course, in the ideas of the Upanishads and later Hindu thought, where it is affirmed that the *atman* (the soul) and *brahman* (the eternal, the principle of creation) are one. Emerson and other members of the Transcendental Club, which he organized, were familiar with the Upanishads, and drew on them as one of their sources of inspiration. Emerson coined his own term for the universal *brahman*, which was one with the self and nature. He called it the 'Over-Soul' – the ultimate authority which transcends the intellect, the link between the *atman* and the *paramatman* (the divine Soul). As Emerson said, 'The simplest person, who in his integrity worships God, becomes God'.[3]

For Emerson therefore each individual, being one with God and nature, had equal access to divinity. The individual was supremely important, and Emerson deplored the excesses of those who claimed to have special revelations from God. Nevertheless, he did not rule out the idea that certain people are acclaimed for specially perceptive insights into the nature of reality, and who can offer guidance to their fellow humans: Emerson called such people 'representative men', and specially singled out Plato (the philosopher), Montaigne (the sceptic), Shakespeare (the poet), Swedenborg (the mystic),

Napoleon (the man of the world) and Goethe (the writer). Jesus was a 'representative man' too, although to claim this status for Jesus is of course not to acknowledge him as anything more than a human being: the characteristics that Jesus possessed are no different from our own, the only difference being that other human beings have a lower degree of receptivity and awareness.

Since nature was the only true teacher, Emerson believed that little was achievable through academic debate, and he therefore tended to avoid it himself. Learning was a matter of intuition, and if he was ever challenged about any of his ideas, Emerson's sole proof was that 'it was instinct'.[4] At the end of one of his lectures, a member of the audience sought him out, and attempted to pose a number of criticisms of his ideas. Emerson's reply was, 'Mr –, if anything I have spoken this evening met your mood, it is well; if it did not, I must tell you that I never argue on these high questions.'[5]

Emerson is important in the development of Unitarianism for several reasons. First, his emphasis on nature and direct access to the *paramatman* was an important break from the arid rationalism that had been characteristic of the history of the movement and of the Enlightenment. Unitarianism had originally been characterized by debates about the nature of the Trinity, the substantiality of the Holy Spirit, the atonement, eternal punishment, and so on. Emerson brought to the movement an important experiential dimension, causing his supporters to recognize that an adequate religion was not merely one that was intellectually sound, but one in which one was enabled to find God for oneself, through nature and through one's own soul.

Second, Emerson was one of the first Unitarians to introduce ideas from other religions, principally Hinduism. He tended to use the ideas of the Upanishads and the Bhagavad Gita, rather than to analyse them, undertake authentic exegesis, or expound them systematically. Emerson was one of the first Unitarians to steer the denomination away from an exclusively Christian standpoint and to move towards a position in which all the major world religions are valued, and credited with important insights into religious truth.

The world-affirming nature of Emerson's philosophy, and its emphasis on enjoying and learning from the natural world, has filtered down into New Age thought. Emerson would no doubt have been attracted by those New Agers in South-West England who want to swim with dolphins and learn from them. Like the present-day New Agers, Emerson exudes an optimism, not only about nature itself, but about the human beings who inhabit the physical world. In common with the New Age movement, Emerson used what we now call the right hand side of the brain, and radically questioned the ability of unaided reason to enable the seeker to arrive at truth – particularly spiritual truth. Emerson was anti-intellectual and anti-establishment, radically questioning the role of traditional institutions such as universities and churches to mediate knowledge of the divine.

Like the present-day New Ager, Emerson was eclectic, not confining himself to the scriptures of any one religious tradition such as Christianity, but combining the insights of the Judaeo-Christian Bible with the Upanishads, the Bhagavad-Gita, his experiences of nature, and some of his dreams. No doubt if a wider variety of religious writings had been available to him, he would have drawn on them also.

Within the denomination today, there are those who seek after a spirituality that dwells on nature. In Britain and in the USA some Unitarians have simultaneously regarded themselves as 'pagans'. Critics sometimes construe 'paganism' as a movement which is opposed to religion. However, those Unitarian pagans will justly point out that the neo-pagan movement stresses the maternal aspect of divinity, which can be seen reflected in the earth ('mother nature'), and hence paganism is a world-affirming 'mother goddess' cult.

In the light of common misconceptions about the term 'pagan' the British Unitarian neo-pagans changed their name to New Age Unitarians, although many pagans outside the denomination would insist that 'paganism' and 'New Age' are not the same at all. In actual fact, the British New Age

Unitarians tend to focus on earth-centred spirituality and celebrating pagan festivals, rather than the wider New Age interests of alternative therapies, crystals, tarot cards and the like.

Just as Emerson could be critical of established practices such as the Lord's Supper, the fact that some belief or practice was novel did not necessarily make it preferable to him. Indeed, he was critical of several innovatory 'alternative' ideas of some of his contemporaries. In an essay entitled 'Demonology', as well as elsewhere, he comes down very heavily on proponents of 'animal magnetism, omens, spiritism [and] mesmerism', all of which were 'fringe' forms of spirituality during the 19th century.[6]

PSYCHICAL RESEARCH

We have seen how Unitarians have always been keen to extend humankind's knowledge and to explore new areas of enquiry. One area which has aroused popular curiosity in recent times has been the paranormal. On both sides of the Atlantic there are Unitarian societies which act as a denominational focus for study of the paranormal.

In Britain, the Unitarian Society for Psychical Studies (USPS) was founded in 1966. Its original aims included the study of 'real or supposed' psychic phenomena in a 'fair and objective' way. Membership is around 200, with an annual conference attracting between 25 and 30 people. It publishes a journal and owns a small library of books and video-tapes. Its range of interest spans telepathy, spiritual healing, precognition, dreams, poltergeists, dowsing, psychic art, out-of-the-body and near-death experiences, mediums, automatic writing, reincarnation and 'far memory' (direct memory of previous lives).

It is significant that the USPS's aims contain the words 'real or supposed' and 'fair and objective'. Membership does not demand that one accepts the authenticity of paranormal phenomena, or that there are only supernatural explanations for such occurrences. However, it would be true to say that, perhaps understandably, its members tend to be sympathetic to their possibility, and a number actually claim to have made contact with the 'other side' or in some other ways to have experienced 'more things in heaven and earth ... than are dreamt of in your philosophy'. I have not come across 'debunkers' amongst Unitarian 'psychics': these are more likely to be found amongst Unitarian humanists.

The three-fold principle of 'freedom, reason and tolerance' tends to cause Unitarian sympathizers to steer a middle course between credulity and paranoia. They differ, on the one hand, from typical attendees of events such as psychic fairs, who uncritically presuppose the veracity of the demonstrators, and encourage active participation in fortune-telling, tarot reading, psychic portrait painting and the like. The USPS is more interested in study than demonstration, and would in no circumstances wish the unwary to dabble with ouija boards or seances.

Some of the 'psychics' would claim that in their studies and experiences of the paranormal they have found evidence that the human soul or spirit survives death. Unitarianism has had no distinctive doctrine of the after-life. One American introduction to Unitarianism states categorically that, 'Very few UUs believe in a continuing individualized existence after physical death'.[7] This may well be true of American Unitarianism, but I doubt if this is the case in Britain and in Eastern Europe. A few Unitarians might expect some better life after this one; some believe in reincarnation, while others may suspend judgement.

As far as the story of Jesus' resurrection is concerned, some Unitarians have believed that Jesus rose from the dead and that his tomb was empty. R V Holt talks about the 'riddle of the empty tomb', for instance.[8] Some have speculated that Jesus acquired a 'subtle body', perhaps akin to the kinds of bodies explored by psychic researchers, while other Unitarians – probably the majority – would regard the doctrine as a myth.

ATHEISTS, AGNOSTICS, HUMANISTS AND TRINITARIANS

In a recent survey carried out within the Glasgow Unitarians it was discovered that out of 35 members, only 8 described

THE EDGES OF TOLERANCE

themselves as 'Christians'. Two claimed the title 'theists', four 'deists', one atheist, two agnostics, eight 'universalists', two 'humanists' and one 'pantheist'. (The remaining seven gave various self-descriptions which do not readily fit into these categories.)[9]

Given the Unitarians' interest in other faiths, it is perhaps not surprising to find the occasional Buddhist within its ranks. In the USA, there is a UU Buddhist Fellowship, which aims to study Buddhist teachings and explore some of its practices. The presence of atheists, agnostics and humanists, however, may seem more surprising. While some Unitarian congregations are more traditionally 'Christian' than others, there is no reason to believe that the Glasgow findings are untypical. One of the Plymouth congregation's most loyal members and office-bearers is a self-avowed atheist!

Some Unitarians have at first found it difficult to admit that they cannot believe in God, and only with difficulty have 'come out' into the open. There need be no embarrassment about doing so, however: if Unitarianism is truly a faith without a creed, it can hardly make classical theism a credal tenet.

Disbelief in God takes a variety forms, and Unitarian atheists may have different reasons for rejecting theism. For some, the God whose existence they reject is the warrior-God of the ancient Hebrew scriptures, a god of wrath, who metes out vengeance to his foes, and demands complete unquestioning obedience, on pain of destruction. For many who view God in this way, God is morally repugnant and certainly not worthy of the praise and adulation that are given in the majority of churches. Some Unitarians may find the existence of God difficult to reconcile with the suffering in the world, while others may feel that there is insufficient evidence in the first place for belief in God's existence to be reasonable.

For some Unitarian atheists, then, their position may in reality be little different from that of the more *avant garde* theologians within Protestant Christianity. For some, their atheism may amount to no more than a rejection of the notion of a God who is 'a person' – someone who is a disembodied mind, but capable of thought, will and action, a God who is a human soul writ large, but of course without any human limitations or imperfections. To many, that kind of God is simply incredible, and some Unitarian atheists will feel that it is more honest to say that they do not believe in God, rather than that they adopt a new model of God, such as 'ultimate reality', 'the ground of our being', an 'impersonal' God who is a force pervading the universe. Intellectual integrity has always been supremely important for Unitarians, and hence it is understandable that some Unitarian atheists will view mainstream theological developments (such as those of Tillich, John Robinson and Don Cupitt)[10] as intellectual gymnastics which are designed to avoid an honest acknowledgement that the God of traditional Judaeo-Christianity simply does not exist.

As far as the presence of self-confessed atheists and agnostics is concerned, the creedless nature of Unitarianism does not exclude them, provided that they can share in the ideals of freedom, reason and tolerance which Unitarianism champions, and the respect for the intrinsic worth of humanity which is implicit in Unitarian philosophy. What they gain from attending worship and participating in the life of the Church is up to each individual, and there is no expectation that an atheist or agnostic would be led to experience God, nor is there any suggestion that they are second-rate citizens on the ground that a God is absent from their world view.

Some atheists and agnostics who attend the Unitarian Church would say that they enjoyed the atmosphere of the services, and shared the common concern for humanity which is expressed within the denomination. For some agnostics Unitarianism offers a free and supportive environment in which to explore, and perhaps in due time reach a conclusion about whether there is a God, and what his, her or its character might be.

As far as the humanist presence is concerned, this should really be no surprise. In fact one prominent Unitarian writer stated, 'No higher authority is given under heaven than the authority in the innermost spirit of man. It is the source of inspiration, the agency of God's revelation to man'.[11] Humanism takes two basic forms: secular and religious. The religious humanist, while not rejecting God's existence, affirms the worth of human beings and the importance of promoting their well-being.

There is much in traditional Unitarianism that lends itself to humanism. From its very origins, Unitarians have emphasized the worth of humanity, rather than embraced Augustinian and Calvinistic doctrines of original sin. While Unitarians cannot but acknowledge that men and women are perfectly capable of selfishness, fraud, aggression and greed, it would be one-sided and unduly pessimistic to focus on the dark side of human nature, as the Calvinists do, rather than on what humanity is capable of becoming.

Humanism has been implicit, too, in the way in which Unitarians have viewed the 'incarnation'. In the mainstream Christian interpretation, only Christ partook simultaneously of godhead and humanity to their full degree. As we have seen, Unitarians have traditionally been uncomfortable with this dogma, stressing the humanity of Jesus. This does not entail (as is often supposed) that they deny Jesus' divinity. On the contrary, many Unitarians are quite comfortable with the assertion that Jesus is 'Son of God', but they typically insist that we are all sons and daughters of God, as the Bible affirms. The quality of Jesus' life probably entailed that he was very considerably more God-like than anyone who has lived ever since, but the difference in god-likeness between oneself and Jesus Christ is a matter of degree. It is not the case that we categorically are not divine, and that Jesus is; rather, there are degrees of divinity.

Unitarians have preached a 'universalized incarnation'.[12] Traditionally, incarnationalists have emphasized the notion that 'God became human', and by so doing have made the doctrine appear somewhat unidirectional. Unitarians would prefer to see the incarnation implying that, with the birth of Jesus Christ, a human became divine. The humanity of any individual entails the possibility of raising that life beyond the worldly material dimension to partake of divinity.

If humanity is divine, then this provides an overwhelming reason for seeing in each individual something of infinite worth, and treating everyone accordingly. For many Unitarians this recognition is the driving force behind their social and humanitarian concerns. As God says in Jesus' parable of the Last Judgement, 'Whatever you did for one of the least of these brothers of mine, you did for me' (Matthew 25.40).

Finally, it is worth mentioning that, since Unitarianism is a faith without a creed, it offers no bar to those who claim to believe that God is three persons in one. One may be tempted to ask why anyone who believes in the Trinity should wish to join a Unitarian congregation, but it does happen! Some who are able to believe in the Trinity may still find the lack of credal constraint appealing; others may have a dual membership, perhaps supporting their local parish church as well as the Unitarians. In Ireland, many members are Trinitarian, but have other reasons for being unable to subscribe to the Westminster Confession. The threefold principle 'freedom, reason and tolerance' enables each member to decide how best to organize his or her religious life.

9 · A Faith with a Future

This book has had much to say about the rich legacy of Unitarian history. Unitarians have sometimes been accused of dwelling too much on their past, but, more to the point, what kind of future can the movement expect?

The denomination is small, and in some parts of the world numbers are declining. The UUA of North America has 150,000 adult members, including about 6,000 in Canada. In Britain there are roughly 7,000 members and 800 children. The Non-Subscribing Presbyterian Church of Ireland (NSPCI) has approximately 3,700 members and 800 children, many of whom regard themselves as Unitarians. Transylvania boasts the largest community of Unitarians for whom English is not their first language, totalling around 80,000. Smaller numbers can be found in Australia (300), South Africa (200) and New Zealand (80).

One British Unitarian booklet, however, is confidently entitled, *Unitarianism – a faith with a future*, and, at the time of writing, British Unitarianism is seeing signs of a slight increase in membership and attendance. Being realistic, it seems likely that Unitarianism will continue to be a minority religion, the majority of the West's population preferring either evangelical Christianity or secularism, with many liberal Christians still feeling that they can be accommodated within mainstream denominations.

It is hard to tell whether Unitarianism is about to see growth, further decline, or equilibrium. It is possible that in Britain and some other European countries, religious affiliation has hit rock bottom, and will experience a gradual upturn: there is certainly some evidence of 'implicit religion', which perhaps inspires confidence that religion, even in its institutionalized forms, is by no means dead. It is possible that, as education improves, there will be greater demands for a 'religion of reason', whose members are encouraged to question, and not merely find glib and spurious answers to deep, and perhaps unanswerable, questions.

If Unitarianism attracts more than its fair share of 'intellectuals', this has its drawbacks. How can Unitarianism reach those who have not had the benefit of a good education? Indeed, *is* Unitarianism likely to appeal to those who have not been to college or university? This question is beginning to exercise the minds of present-day Unitarians, and formed the subject of one of the seminars I attended at the UUA General Assembly at Spokane in 1995. While Unitarians are keen to attract new attendees from all walks of life, they certainly would not wish to downgrade their religion to a simple – not to say, simplistic – faith like that of the Christian evangelicals, and to dispense neat answers to complex and controversial problems. For this reason, it seems likely that Unitarianism will continue to attract those who wish to reflect on the deeper issues relating to God and the universe, rather than those who believe they have already found all their answers.

CHRISTIAN, MULTI-FAITH OR HUMANIST?

All religious communities develop in the course of time and, perhaps more than most, Unitarianism is ready to accept change and to move on. In the USA and Britain the multi-faith interest looks set to remain, and indeed it is difficult to see how things could be otherwise. Given the overwhelming belief in freedom, reason and tolerance, it seems unlikely that

Unitarianism would ever backtrack on its acknowledgement of the inner lights of reason and conscience that potentially exist in all peoples, cultures and religions.

The interest in world religions has shifted from theoretical interest and mutual dialogue to a stage where the Unitarian movement has drawn on them for spiritual edification. Modern Unitarian hymnals, for example, now contain material culled from a variety of world religious traditions. The UUA hymnal, *Singing the Living Tradition*, which was brought out in 1993, contains substantial contributions derived from all the major world traditions, which can be sung or read during worship. In Britain one Unitarian minister, John Storey (b1935), has translated pieces of Buddhist writing into hymns. His poem, 'True Religion', is a translation of the words of the present Dalai Lama, and sums up well the Unitarian perspective on belief and practice:

> Religion needs to permeate
> The common life of every day;
> Each to the other must relate
> To build the world for which we pray.
>
> Our forms and customs will not meet
> The spirit's needs we deeply feel,
> Unless our hearts with quickened beat
> Match outward show with inner zeal.
>
> When thoughts are pure, and words are kind,
> Compassionate our every deed,
> With selfishness put from the mind
> Our lives become a worthy creed.[1]

One area in which there has recently been growing interest has been 'earth-centred' spirituality. The increasing interest in paganism, 'goddess spirituality' and Native American religion amongst spiritual seekers in the West has been shared by UUs in the USA and Canada. In Canada in particular, many Unitarians have been pleased to affirm the spiritual legacy of the Canadian Indian, since the Indian tradition permeates Canadian culture. In 1995, at the UUA

General Assembly at Spokane, it was decided to amend the UUA Principles, which had acknówledged Christianity, Judaism, 'the world's religions' and humanism as sources of inspiration, to include an acknowledgement that UUs drew inspiration from 'Spiritual teachings of Earth-centered traditions which celebrate the sacred circle of life and instruct us to live in harmony with the rhythms of nature'.[2]

Whether or not they are interested in earth-centred spirituality, most members would share a concern for the earth and for the future of the planet. Most, if not all churches, not only have members who are actively supporting environmental organizations, but also try to ensure that they use environmentally friendly and fairly traded goods.

The increased interest in world religions has caused some Unitarians on both sides of the Atlantic to believe that there is a danger of the denomination casting its spiritual net too wide, and losing track of its historical origins and tradition, which – as we have seen – are firmly within Protestant Christianity. Accordingly the Unitarian Christian Association was recently formed in Britain (a sister organization already existed in the USA). These Associations are by no means hostile to the religious pluralism which has become characteristic of the Unitarian movement, but merely seek to ensure that, given the variety of sources of inspiration, the Christian tradition is not lost or obscured.

The multi-faith interest has largely passed Eastern European Unitarians by. This is partly because the area is geographically remote from the West, and is largely non-English-speaking: hence ideas from other religions traditions cannot so readily be disseminated. A further inhibiting factor has been the fact that Hungary and Romania have only recently emerged from a 40-year period of communist oppression. During that time, church properties were confiscated and serious restrictions placed on church activities: for example, in Romania, only a small government-imposed quota of ministerial candidates was allowed to train at the Unitarian seminary in Kolozsvár (Cluj). Following the removal of Ceauşescu in 1990, the Romanian Church has focused on renewing its former strength, attempting to regain its property, and securing the training of larger numbers of ministerial candidates. Even with the demise of communism, Transylvanian Unitarians still find themselves a minority, being largely Hungarian-speaking in a country where Romanian is the official language. Retaining their ethnic identity is therefore an important issue.

Given this situation, it is understandable that Hungarian and Romanian Unitarians should look to their past tradition, which they are still in the process of repossessing, rather than to any future which might entail innovation and change. For some of the younger ministerial students, however, their countries' new-found freedom has provided the chance to travel and to undergo part of their training in Britain and the USA. Some have encountered the innovations which I have mentioned, and have expressed a desire to introduce new forms of worship back in the Unitarian villages. However, rural Unitarians tend to be conservative, and to be justly proud of the legacy of heroes such as Francis Dávid, and committed to very traditional forms of worship which are firmly within the Christian mould. It is very doubtful whether, at least in the foreseeable future, they would be willing to see their faith develop along similar lines to Britain, the USA and Canada.

SERVICE TO HUMANITY

I have already mentioned the interest in humanism on the part of some Unitarians, on both sides of the Atlantic. This seems likely to continue, and a number of Unitarian ministers have attracted the label 'humanist', with corresponding implications regarding their style of ministry. In some of these 'humanist' congregations, it can be difficult to find a Bible, which may seldom feature in worship, where more attention would typically be given to extolling the virtues of human endeavour, and preparing oneself for the service of humanity.

There are some signs that the Christian and the humanist ends of the Unitarian spectrum are not as far apart as they once seemed. When I attended the UUA General Assembly in

1995, some participants commented on how the Unitarian humanists were beginning to use words like 'soul' once again, which formerly they avoided. Equally, those Unitarians who regard themselves as Christians would not deny that men and women are created in God's image, and that true worship of God entails respect and concern for one's fellow human beings.

On matters of human relationships, one interesting recent development in the area of sexual equality has been the recent formation of the UU Men's Network ('UUMen' as it is called) in America. Formed in 1993, UUMen aims to encourage men to examine their masculine attitudes, particularly with regard to sexual and social justice. UUMen acknowledges that society's male-dominated past has seen the rise and continuation of many forms of injustice, prejudice and discrimination, and that, if these wrongs are to be healed, men must examine and change their attitudes. UUMen's purpose is 'to build a positive liberal religious masculinity: male-positive, pro-feminist/womanist, gay-affirming, culturally and racially inclusive and diverse' (UUMen leaflet, 1995). If all this sounds unduly serious, branches of UUMen do organize social events, poetry readings, and the like; formal membership is restricted to men, but women can affiliate as supporting members.

It is one thing for a denomination to express its commitment to an ideal, but quite another matter to live up to and achieve it. For instance, in most denominations where women are eligible for the ministry, they are still in a definite minority. Although it is relatively easy to affirm gay and lesbian rights, and racial equality, it is much more difficult to reflect these ideals representatively in one's institutional structures.

The end of the 20th century has seen near equality of the sexes in the Unitarian ministry. Approximately half of the Unitarian ministers in the USA are women, and in Britain about a third. Two-thirds of American ministerial candidates are currently women – a great advance from even 20 years ago, when the norm was 1 in 10. In Britain the Presidency of the General Assembly – a post with a new occupant each year – interchanges equally between men and woman, and between ministers and lay people.

As far as the blessing of gay partnerships is concerned, Unitarians maintain their tradition of devising services of worship to suit the special needs of members and others who seek specific and often personal religious rites. Gay blessings are fairly commonplace in Unitarian circles in the USA. Meanwhile in Britain, Andrew Hill's book of services, *Celebrating Life*, includes one specimen service to serve such a purpose. At present, many Unitarian congregations still need to be persuaded that such rituals are appropriate, although I do know Unitarian ministers who have presided at such ceremonies. A handful of ministers live with same-sex partners: this is tolerated, but it has to be said that many Unitarians still do not welcome such arrangements. Prejudice remains, and it is to be hoped that the 21st century will see a greater tolerance for those who have sexual orientations which are, after all, not of their choice.

It has been a little more difficult to attract 'people of colour' to Unitarianism, and particularly to the ministry. To some degree this is understandable since, in the days of immigration, people brought their own religion with them. It is unlikely that the immigrants of the late 1950s and early 1960s in Britain would convert away from Islam, Sikhism and Hinduism (the three most common immigrant faiths), nor would Unitarians wish them to do so. Equally, the Afro-Caribbean communities have brought with them Black Pentecostalism and Rastafarianism. Nevertheless, American Unitarianism has seen a drive for Afro-Americans to study for the ministry, with subsidies for their training.

The USA has begun to see a change in the concept of ministry itself, and the concept of a 'community minister' is a recent innovation. The community minister is somewhat analogous to the Roman Catholic 'worker priest', who carries out work which many might regard as secular employment, but who makes it a ministry. In the UUA, community ministries primarily include social work and counselling, work to which such ministers are formally ordained, and which is paid for and supported by the denomination. Future years may well see some growth and spread of this type of ministry.

113

THE ADVANCE OF SCIENCE

One phenomenon of the 21st century will undoubtedly be continued scientific and technological progress. Having no creeds to be dented by unfavourable counter-evidence, Unitarianism has always welcomed scientific progress, never seeing this as a threat to religious doctrine, but as important advances in our understanding of the universe. While mainstream Christianity has still not fully recovered from Darwin and the theory of evolution, Unitarians would not be unduly worried by claims (of which there are some) that the discovery of fish fossils on mountain tops confirms the biblical story of the flood, showing that creationists are more worthy of credence than the evolutionists. Although most Unitarians today would tend to support evolutionism, this is not part of their creed, and if the balance of evidence supported a contrary view, Unitarians would be happy to consider it, and see where it led.

Unitarianism has also endeavoured to keep up with modern technology, and to use it to best advantage. The advent of the Internet has afforded new ways for the denomination and for members to disseminate and exchange ideas. Consistent with its policy of catering for people's special needs, Unitarianism has for some decades tried to assist those who have been physically isolated from a congregation, either because they are geographically too distant, or because of some disability that prevents them from attending worship on a Sunday, or joining other congregational activities.

Being a relatively small but geographically far-flung denomination, there are inevitably Unitarians who find themselves isolated and unable to communicate directly with other like-minded people. In the USA and Canada the 'Church of the Larger Fellowship' sends out a monthly publication, *Quest*, which provides sermons, meditations, resources for living and material for children, to cater for those who cannot attend worship on a regular basis.

In Britain, the National Unitarian Fellowship (NUF) is somewhat more interactive. Apart from conventional forms of communication, such as a newsletter and annual conferences, members can communicate by means of Books of Fellowship and Tapes of Fellowship. These start life blank, and are circulated around small groups of members, who add their thoughts on a selected theme, and pass the book or tape on to someone else.

Outside the NUF, a number of E-mail discussion groups, run for the Hibbert Trust by a Unitarian minister in Britain, exchange questions, comments and information from all parts of the globe. Two groups focus on matters of Unitarian interest, while another is concerned with rites. In this third group, subscribers can exchange information about forms of worship and, particularly, services that are particularly geared to the special needs of individuals. Gay couples might seek guidance about how to celebrate their union; someone may be looking for a reading or a poem to suit a special theme; a funeral may be needed for a suicide victim; on one occasion a student sought and received suggestions for a dissertation on 'flowers and religion'. At present, only a minority of Unitarians are connected to the Internet, so the more traditional ways of communication still play an important role in the British NUF.

WHAT WILL 21ST CENTURY UNITARIANISM BE LIKE?

What will Unitarianism be like in the next century? The last hundred years have certainly seen vast changes in the denomination. Unitarian leaders of a century ago, such as Jenkin Lloyd Jones, James Martineau, Olympia Brown or Gertrud von Petzold would scarcely recognize present-day Unitarianism as the denomination to which they belonged. Whether they would have welcomed the changes is anyone's guess, but Unitarians can certainly be sure that the next century will see developments that may alter it out of all recognition.

It is always tempting to end a book with a little crystal-gazing, when it is usually impossible to predict what the future will bring. I would hazard a few guesses, however. The present interest in world religions, which has developed particularly in the past hundred years, is likely to continue. As is their practice, Unitarians will not seek to convert their followers to their own brand of religion. Not only would that be at odds with the principles of 'freedom, reason and tolerance', but Unitarianism can only thrive where there exists a variety of traditions on which to draw.

As far as proselytizing is concerned, Unitarians in Britain are becoming aware that they are hiding their light under a bushel, and that attempts at publicizing the denomination are no bad thing. If there is slight growth in future years, this is likely to come from those who are currently 'unchurched', and a few who come to be disenchanted with the dogmatism of much mainstream religion.

It is difficult to determine whether the New Age is merely a passing interest, or whether it is here to stay. Certainly there is a growing demand, both inside and outside the Unitarian movement, for a spirituality which does more than satisfy the intellect. Some Unitarians may find this in earth-centred spirituality, or in New Age philosophy, but we may well see more widely a renewed interest in prayer, meditation and the spiritual life.

Most importantly, Unitarian churches will continue to provide an environment for those who feel that they are inherently 'religious', but who have doubts which they are less able to share in other religious arenas. For those who wish to develop their own religious view of life, Unitarianism will continue to provide the framework in which to do so. For such people at least, Unitarianism is certainly 'a faith with a future'.

NOTES AND REFERENCES

CHAPTER 1

1 Erdö, John, *Transylvanian Unitarian Church: Chronological History and Theological Essays,* Chico, CA: The Center for Free Religion, p47, 1990
2 Parke, David B (ed), *The Epic of Unitarianism: Original Writings from the History of Liberal Religion,* Boston: Skinner House p26, 1957, 1985
3 The Arians will be explained on p28

CHAPTER 2

1 Wilbur, E M, *A History of Unitarianism in Transylvania, England and America*, Cambridge, Mass: Harvard University Press, p396, 1952
2 Parke, op cit, p113
3 Wilbur, op cit, p463
4 Ibid, p474
5 Ibid, p483
6 Howe, Charles A, *The Larger Faith: A Short History of American Universalism*, Boston: Skinner House, p60, 1993
7 Ibid, p18

CHAPTER 3

1 Hill, Andrew M, *The Unitarian Path*, London: Lindsey Press, p5, 1994
2 Westminster Confession, XIV: vii
3 By L Griswold Williams
4 Unitarian Universalist Association, Article II; Principles and Purposes, Section C-2.1 Principles

CHAPTER 4

1 See Chapter 5

CHAPTER 5

1 Martineau, James, *The Seat of Authority in Religion*, London: Longmans, Green & Co, p521, 1890
2 Smith, R Gregor, *Secular Christianity* London: Collins, p103, 1966
3 *Hymns of Faith & Freedom*, London: Chalice Press, no215, v3, 1991

CHAPTER 6

1 Spears, R et al, *Memorable Unitarians*, London: British and Foreign Unitarian Association, p202, 1906
2 Roy, Rammohun, *Final Appeal to the Christian Public, In Defence of the 'Precepts of Jesus'*, Calcutta: Unitarian Press, pp349–50 London edition, 1823
3 Carpenter, J Estlin, 1893, 'Wider Views of Revelation', in Barrows, J H (ed), *The World's Parliament of Religions*, Chicago: The Parliament Publishing Company, Vol II, p848, 1893
4 Jones, Jenkin Lloyd, 1891, 'The Creedless Church', quoted in Braybrooke, M, *Pilgrimage of Hope*, London: SCM, p17, 1992
5 Braybrooke, op cit, p40
6 Chryssides, G D, *The Path of Buddhism*, Edinburgh: St Andrew Press, p144, 1988

7 Braybrooke, op cit, p48
8 The General Assembly of Unitarian and Free Christian Churches, *Handbook*, London: Unitarian Headquarters, p71, 1986
9 Sias, John, *100 Questions that Non-Members Ask about Unitarian Universalism*, Nashua, New Hampshire: Transition Publishing, p6, 1995
10 Lovis, Richard, *Plymouth Unitarian Church Calendar*, December 1994

CHAPTER 7

1 Packard, V, The Waste Makers, London: Longmans Green and Co, p177, 1961
2 Wright, Conrad, *A Stream of Light: A Short History of American Unitarianism*, Boston: Skinner House Books, p42, 1975, 1989
3 Holt, Raymond V, *The Unitarian Contribution to Social Progress in England*, London: Lindsey Press, p20, 1938, 1952

CHAPTER 8

1 Holt, op cit, p67
2 Emerson; quoted in Wright, op cit, p46
3 Lash, John, *The Seeker's Handbook: The Complete Guide to Spiritual Pathfinding*, New York: Harmony Books, pp385–6, 1990
4 Geldard, Richard, *The Esoteric Emerson: The Spiritual Teachings of Ralph Waldo Emerson*, Hudson, NY: Lindisfarne Press, p81, 1993
5 Quoted in ibid, p32
6 Ibid, pp115-16
7 op cit, p4, 1995
8 Holt, Raymond V et al, *A Free Religious Faith: The Report of a Unitarian Commission*, London: Lindsey Press, p123, 1945, 1960
9 *The Inquirer*, no7282, 7 March 1992, p6
10 All three writers denied believing in a God 'out there', but continued to use language about God.

THE ELEMENTS OF UNITARIANISM

11 Holt et al, p82
12 Ibid, p126

CHAPTER 9

1 *Hymns for Living*, London: Lindsey Press, no189, 1985
2 UUA Principles, Section C-2.1

FURTHER READING

Adams, James Luther, *The Prophethood of All Believers*, Boston: Beacon Press, 1986

Barr, Margaret, *A Dream Come True: The Story of Kharang*, London: Lindsey Press, 1974

Bartlett, Laile E and Bartlett, Josiah, *A Religion for the 'Non-Religious': An Overview of Unitarian Universalism*, Berkeley, California: L E and J R Bartlett, 1990

Bolam, C Gordon et al, *The English Presbyterians from Elizabethan Puritanism to Modern Unitarianism*, London: George Allen & Unwin, 1968

Braybrooke, Marcus, *Pilgrimage of Hope: One Hundred Years of Global Interfaith Dialogue*, London: SCM Press, 1992

Clarke, James Freeman, *Ten Great Religions: An Essay in Comparative Theology*, Boston: Houghton, Osgood and Company, 1879

Drummond, W H (ed), *The Book of the Hibbert Trust*, London: The Hibbert Trust, 1933

Erdö, John, *Transylvanian Unitarian Church: Chronological History and Theological Essays*, Chico, CA: The Center for Free Religion, 1990

Geldard, Richard, *The Esoteric Emerson: The Spiritual Teachings of Ralph Waldo Emerson*, Hudson, NY: Lindisfarne Press, 1993

Gleadle, Kathryn, *The Early Feminists: Radical Unitarians and the Emergence of the Women's Rights Movement, 1831–51*, New York: St Martin's Press, 1995

Gordon, Alexander, *Heads of English Unitarian History: with appended lectures on Baxter and Priestley*, Portway, Bath: Cedric Chivers, 1895,1970

Goring, J and Goring, R, *The Unitarians*, Exeter: Religious and Moral Education Press, 1984

Gow, Henry, *The Unitarians*, London: Methuen, 1928

Hall, Alfred, *The Beliefs of a Unitarian*, London: The Lindsey Press, 1932

Hewett, Phillip, *The Unitarian Way*, Toronto: Canadian Unitarian Council, 1985

Hewett, Phillip, *Understanding Unitarians*, London: The Hibbert Trust, 1992

Hill, Andrew M, *Celebrating Life: a Book of Special Services*, London: Lindsey Press, 1993

Hill, Andrew M, *The Unitarian Path*, London: The Lindsey Press & Unitarians in Edinburgh, 1994

Holt, Raymond V, *The Unitarian Contribution to Social Progress in England*, London: The Lindsey Press 1938, 1952

Holt, Raymond V et al, *A Free Religious Faith: The Report of a Unitarian Commission*, London: The Lindsey Press, 1945, 1960

Hostler, John, *Unitarianism*, London: The Hibbert Trust, 1981

Howe, Charles A, *The Larger Faith: A Short History of American Universalism*, Boston: Skinner House Books, 1993

Jefferson, Thomas, *The Jefferson Bible*, Boston: Beacon Press, 1904, 1989

Kingston, A Richard, *God in One Person: The Case for Non-Incarnational Christianity*, London: Macmillan, 1993

Lange, Fred E Jr, *Famous Unitarians/Universalists*, Garwood, NJ: Fred E Lange Jr, 1981, 1991

Lash, John, *The Seeker's Handbook: The Complete Guide to Spiritual Pathfinding*, New York: Harmony Books, 1990

Lavan, Spencer, *Unitarians and India: A Study in Encounter and Response*, Chicago: Exploration Press, 1991

McLachlan, H, *The Unitarian Movement in the Religious Life of England*, London: George Allen and Unwin, 1934

McLachlan H J, *Socinianism in 17th Century England*, Oxford: Oxford University Press, 1951

Marshall, George N, *Challenge of a Liberal Faith*, Boston: Skinner House Books, 1966, 1991

Martineau, James, *The Seat of Authority in Religion*, London: Longmans, Green & Co, 1890

Parke, David B (ed), *The Epic of Unitarianism: Original Writings from the History of Liberal Religion*, Boston: Skinner House Books, 1957, 1985

Robinson, David, *The Unitarians and the Universalists*, Westport and London: Greenwood Press, 1985

Ruston, Alan R, *The Hibbert Trust: A History*, London: The Hibbert Trust, 1984

Sargant, Norman C, *Mary Carpenter in India*, Bristol: A J Sargant, 1987

Schulz, William F (ed), *The Unitarian Universalist Pocket Guide*, Boston: Skinner House Books, 1993

Seaburg, Carl, *The Communion Book*, Boston: Unitarian Universalist Ministers Association, 1993

Sias, John, *100 Questions that Non-Members Ask about Unitarian Universalism*, Nashua, New Hampshire: Transition Publishing, 1995

Spears, R et al, *Memorable Unitarians*, London: British and Foreign Unitarian Association, 1906

Tarrant, W G, *The Story and Significance of the Unitarian Movement*, London: Philip Green, 1910

Wigmore-Beddoes, Dennis G, *Yesterday's Radicals: A Study of the Affinity between Unitarianism and Broad Church Anglicanism in the Nineteenth Century*, Cambridge and London: James Clarke & Co, 1971

Wigmore-Beddoes, Dennis G, *A Religion that Thinks – A Psychological Study: The Psychology of Unitarianism*, Belfast: The Ulster Unitarian Christian Association, 1972

Wilbur, Earl Morse, *A History of Unitarianism: Socinianism and its Antecedents*, Cambridge, Mass: Harvard University Press, 1946

Wilbur, Earl Morse, *A History of Unitarianism In Transylvania, England and America*, Cambridge, Mass: Harvard University Press, 1952

Wright, Conrad Edick, *A Stream of Light: A Short History of American Unitarianism*, Boston: Skinner House Books, 1975, 1989.

Wright, Conrad Edick, *American Unitarianism 1805–1865*, Boston: The Massachusetts Historical Society and Northeastern University Press, 1989

USEFUL ADDRESSES

General Assembly of Unitarian and Free Christian Churches
Essex Hall
1-6 Essex Street, London, WC2R 3HY, England, UK
Telephone: (144) 171 240 2384 Fax: (+44) 171 240 3089
E-mail: ga@unitarian.org.uk

The Unitarian Universalist Association (UUA)
25 Beacon Street, Boston, MA 02108, USA
Telephone: 617 742 2100 Fax: 617 367 3237
E-mail: kmaclean@uua.org

The Canadian Unitarian Council
188 Eglington Avenue East, Toronto, Ontario, M4P 2X7,
Canada.
Telephone: 416 489 4121 Fax: 416 489 9010
E-mail: cuc@web.net

The Unitarian Church of Romania (Transylvania)
3400 Cluj, B-dul 22 Decembrie nc.9, Kolosvar, Cluj, Romania
Telephone: 40 64 195927/193236 Fax: 40 64 195927

The Unitarian Church in Budapest, Hungary
H-1055 Budapest, Nagy Ignac utca 4, Hungary
Telephone/Fax: 36 1 1112801

USEFUL INTERNET SITES

http://www.unitarian.org.uk
Gives information primarily on British Unitarianism.

http://www.uua.org
http://www.unitarian.org/
These connect you to the Unitarian Universalists' site in the USA.

http://www.hibbert.org.uk
The Church of the Open Mind – about liberal religion, with special reference to Unitarianism.

http://www.web.net/~cuc
Canadian Unitarian Council.

INDEX

International Council of UUs
52–3
Internet 8, 82, 114, 115
Ireland 17, 24, 60, 78, 106,
107
Islam 10, 13, 68, 71, 73, 74,
77, 113, 136

Jainism 69, 77
Jefferson, Thomas 81
Jesus Christ
death and resurrection of
29, 36, 40, 41, 59, 61,
63–4, 76, 102
deity of 4, 5, 11, 12–13,
14, 16, 19, 20–21, 24,
27, 28, 30, 36, 40, 44,
63, 64, 79, 105
humanity of 15, 28, 35,
44, 99
teacher and example 7,
14–15, 36, 44, 59, 62,
63, 70, 77, 78, 82, 88,
106
see also atonement;
Christology; non-
adorationism
John, St 42, 43, 72
Jones, Jenkin Lloyd 74, 115
Joy, Charles 94
Jews 6, 10, 13, 44, 68, 74,
77–8, 84, 94,
Judaism 9, 38, 44, 61, 65,
66, 77, 110
justice 41, 45, 46, 55, 94,
112

King, Thomas Starr 35
Kitson, James 91

laity, role of 48–9, 59, 113
Lamb, Charles 82
Lécfalva, Diet of 9
life after death 10, 41, 59,
102
Lindsey, Theophilus 9, 18,
19, 23, 28, 28, 84
Livermore, Mary 91
Locke, John 32, 84
Longfellow, Henry W 82
Luther, Martin 10, 11
Lyell, Charles 21, 82

Manchester College 72, 90
marriage 56, 57, 58–9, 91
Martineau, James 22, 23, 56,
67, 115
Mary, Virgin 10, 15, 18
Matheson, George 66
meditation 55, 114, 116
Melville, Herman 82
membership 57–8, 70, 107
Mennonites 87
Methodism 23
ministry 29, 35, 47–9, 50,
51, 52, 54, 55, 59, 90,
92, 110–13
miracles 15, 21, 32, 41–2,
55, 56, 61, 63, 70, 79, 81
Morse, Jedediah 27, 28,
Morse, Samuel 82
Moses 9, 20, 21
Müller, F Max 69, 75
Murray, John 34–36
Muslims see Islam